Talk It Over!

Talk It Over!

LISTENING, SPEAKING, AND PRONUNCIATION

SECOND EDITION

Joann Rishel Kozyrev

Houghton Mifflin Company Boston New York

Editor in Chief: Patricia A. Coryell

Director of ESL Publishing: Susan Maguire

Senior Development Editor: Kathy Sands Boehmer

Editorial Assistant: Mira Bharin

Senior Project Editor: Kathryn Dinovo

Manufacturing Manager: Florence Cadran

Marketing Manager: Annamarie Rice

Marketing Associate: Claudia Martínez

Cover image: Alexander Papaleo

Photo Credits: Page 1 Ronnie Kaufman/Corbis Stock Market; page 5 Gary Andrashko for Plimoth Plantation; Ted Curtin for Plimoth Plantation; page 19 Shelley Gazin/CORBIS; page 34 Douglas Kirkland/CORBIS; page 37 Thomas H. Brakefield/Corbis Stock Market; page 40 Thomas H. Brakefield/Corbis Stock Market; page 42 The Pensacola News Journal; page 53 Judith Cezar; page 56 Owen Franken/CORBIS; page 58 Jessica Drake; page 69 Richard Heinzen/SuperStock; page 87 Sarah Hoskins; page 90 Christopher Morris/PictureQuest; page 92 Ryan McVay/PhotoDisc; page 107 Chuck Savage/Corbis Stock Market; page 109 Diana Soviero; page 111 David King; page 125 George Shelley/Corbis Stock Market; page 138 Mug Shots/Corbis Stock Market

college.hmco.com

Printed in the U.S.A.

Library of Congress Control Number: 2001131517

ISBN: 0-618-14401-3

23456789-SB-05 04 03 02

Contents

Skills Coverage in Talk It Over!

Chapter	Listening	Note Taking	Pronunciation	Speaking
1: Family	Main ideas Compare and contrast Key terms Details	Basic skills Abbreviations	Thought groups	Discussion skills
2: World Entertainment	Main ideas Details	Listing	Question and statement intonation	Asking and answering questions
3: Environmental Activism	Inference Time order Main ideas	Cause and effect organizational patterns	Syllable stress in compound words and phrasal verbs	Defending an opinion
4: The Sounds of Language	Understand attitudes Details Main ideas	The Cornell method	Rhythm and sentence stress	Definitions
5: Biotechnology	Main ideas Details Time order	Outlining Summarizing from notes	Focal stress	Panel presentation
6: Roots: Living in Two Cultures	Main ideas Details Predictions	Idea mapping	Intonation to signal complete and incomplete thoughts	Presenting to a small group
7: Making it Work	Main ideas Details	Paragraph style	Important endings	Speaking persuasively
8: Alternative Medicine	Main ideas Details Specific words	Getting complete information	Linking and features of fast speech	Formal presentations Fact and opinion

Talk It Over! is designed to be a complete text for the high-intermediate to advanced oral communication classroom. The text provides a framework to help students build both the fluency and the accuracy of their listening and speaking skills. It has been designed to completely integrate listening, speaking, and pronunciation practice, while allowing the teacher the flexibility to choose the elements of the course that the particular students in each class need the most.

The text is based on the following model for the development of oral communication skills.

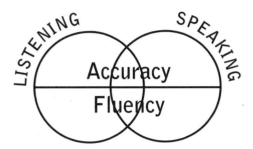

This model demonstrates how listening, speaking, accuracy, and fluency can work together to form the whole that is oral communication. In this model, the listening and speaking skills are represented by two overlapping circles. This illustrates that the skills are inherently related, although they sometimes operate separately. A line through the center of the diagram illustrates the division between accuracy and fluency.

Although accuracy and fluency interconnect, students experience the greatest improvement when they focus on one of these elements in a given activity. This focus provides attainable goals, allows students to build specific skills, offers useful strategies for improvement, and reduces the frustration that many students feel when confronting the difficult task of concentrating simultaneously on meaning, vocabulary, fluency, and accuracy.

Each chapter in *Talk It Over!* includes two complementary listening passages on the same topic. These passages feature authentic, unscripted language in a variety of formats such as interviews, radio documentaries, and lectures. The listening, pronunciation, and speaking activities that students complete are all based on these listening passages, and the models for the pronunciation and speaking skills practiced are taken directly from the listening passages. Listening skills emphasized in this book include listening for main ideas, understanding detail, and note taking. In the pronunciation activities, students focus on understanding the meaning conveyed by suprasegmentals and on producing suprasegmentals to convey meaning. In the sections entitled "Talk It Over!," students practice speaking in academic and professional situations such as discussions, debates, interviews, and oral presentations. The chapters are sequenced so that earlier activities provide support for later activities, but care has been taken to ensure that the chapters and activities can be used in any order. Each chapter is divided into the following sections.

Brainstorming

This section focuses on the segment of the model that represents speaking fluency. In this section, students
- examine and analyze information in charts, graphs, and readings;
- think about the overarching theme of the unit;
- begin to make predictions about the ideas that they will listen to; and
- discuss with others in the class the inferences, ideas, and questions that the information raises for them.

Listening One

Activities in this section focus on the circle in the model that represents listening. The authentic listenings and accompanying exercises for each chapter include activities that
- focus on understanding main ideas and details,
- ask students to interact with the language of the passage,
- emphasize skills such as discerning the meaning of unfamiliar words and understanding analogies, and
- develop critical listening.

Listening Two

The second authentic listening passage provides additional information, a contrasting viewpoint, or a different perspective on the topic from that expressed in the first listening. Listening One and Listening Two are designed to complement each other; however, the passages may be used separately as time and student needs dictate. Listening Two and accompanying activities always include:
- note-taking models to acquaint students with a variety of strategies for taking notes;
- examples in the pronunciation section that are drawn from Listening Two; and
- some follow-up activities that encourage students to compare, contrast, and critically examine the ideas presented in Listening One and Listening Two.

Pronunciation Activities

In this section, activities focus on the segments of the model that represent accuracy in listening and speaking. Each chapter has a pronunciation section that offers

- practice in listening to, understanding, and producing suprasegmentals;
- emphasis on the meaning conveyed by suprasegmentals such as intonation, stress, and pausing;
- examples drawn from the listening passages to provide immediate context for the examples and to allow students to understand the passages on a deeper level; and
- production activities that provide the controlled pronunciation practice of skills linked to the chapter's speaking activities.

Talk It Over!

This section offers extensive speaking activities that develop both fluency and accuracy. The activities draw on the ideas that students listened to in the passages and offer practice in the kinds of communication heard in the listenings. The chapters are arranged so that students receive exposure to and practice with a variety of advanced communication skills necessary in academic and professional situations, including

- participating in discussions,
- conducting interviews,
- presenting to large and small groups, and
- participating in persuasive speaking and debate.

Further Practice

The activities in this section allow students to work on listening and speaking activities at a higher level of complexity. These activities often encourage students to use their listening and speaking skills to interact with other English speakers and to collect and report on information that they have gathered. So that students and instructors can personalize the course to best meet their needs, this section includes activities such as

- readings,
- discussion practice,
- guided television viewing, and
- detailed listening practice.

Web Activities

Talk It Over! has a page on the Houghton Mifflin ESL World Wide Web site, www.college.hmco.com. On this page are activities and links that enable teachers and students to do activities using authentic sources on the Web that are related to the context and skills in each chapter. The activities on the site can be used in the classroom, laboratory, or individual study settings.

Self-Evaluation

Each chapter ends with a self-evaluation chart that can be used by students and teachers to chart the student's progress through the units, identify weaknesses where extra practice is required, and set goals. The chart can be completed as the class progresses through the chapter or at the chapter's end. The evaluation charts are designed so that they can be completed by the students on their own or during meetings with the teacher. The teacher will be able to encourage the discussion of learning styles and preferred strategies based on the students' responses in the charts.

New in the Second Edition

Several improvements have been made to this new edition of *Talk it Over!*. The new edition still contains

- integrated listening, pronunciation, and speaking practice;
- high frequency, interesting topics;
- authentic listenings;
- a variety of speaking skills and strategies; and
- self-evaluations of skills taught in each chapter.

The new edition includes the following new features:

- A chapter on the topic of family
- More thorough, controlled, and communicative pronunciation practice
- Clearer activity direction lines
- Note-taking models
- Improved page layout and design

Acknowledgments

Many people have contributed to the development of *Talk It Over!*. I am especially grateful to the editorial team at Houghton Mifflin: Susan Maguire for her vision and support; Kathleen Sands Boehmer for her encouragement and inspiring guidance; and Manuel Muñoz for his patience and many kindnesses. The interviews and authentic recordings are such an interesting and integral part of this book, I would like to thank Judith Ritter, of Dana Knight Communications, and Phil Lee, of Full House Productions, for collecting this excellent material. Jay Neugeboren and Carol Berkin were kind enough to be interviewed for the new edition, and I am indebted to them for sharing their ideas and thoughts with us. I am grateful to Cindy Johnson and her team for the time and skill they put into creating the design for this edition as well as for researching and finding such ideal photographs and illustrations. My brother, Jay Rishel, and his cable modem also helped a great deal with Internet searches at just the right moment.

Finally, I wish to thank my colleagues, especially Marni Baker Stein, who brought fresh energy and insight to the series both personally and professionally. I am indebted to the teachers and students who used the first edition of this book and gave me valuable feedback. The following reviewers provided their expertise and many useful suggestions:

Heidi Adamson, Northern Virginia Community College

Carolann DeSelms, Marymount College

Kelly H. Gutierrez, University of Texas, Pan American

Janine Rudnick, El Paso Community College

Aija Saario, Georgia Perimeter College

1

Family

Brainstorming

Discuss the following question with others in your class, or record your answer on tape.

Would you rather live in a large family or a small family? What are the advantages of each?

Gathering Information from a Graph

The following graph shows how families in the United States have been changing since the 1970s.[1] Study the chart, and then discuss the questions that follow with others in your class.

Married couple with
children under 18

Married couple with
no children

Single mother with
children under 18

Single father with
children under 18

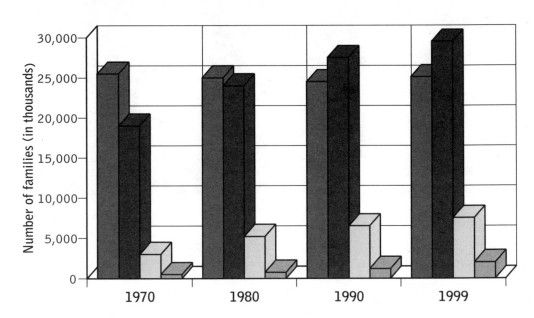

Discussion Questions

1. According to this graph, what kinds of families are becoming more common? Are any kinds of families becoming less common? What do you think the reasons are for these trends?

2. This graph shows only four types of families. What other groups of people do you think can be called a family?

Listening One
Family: A Modern Viewpoint

Jay Neugeboren is a novelist who has written many books. *Imagining Robert* is one of his books, and it is a memoir about his relationship with his younger brother Robert, his brother's mental illness, and the people in their immediate and extended families. We asked him about his family and how his family experience is different from his children's.

Before You Listen

Before you listen to the interview with novelist Jay Neugeboren, talk about the following questions with others in your class.

1. What is your definition of the word "family"? How many people do you think are in a family?

2. Do you know anyone who grew up in an unusually large family? Do you know anyone who grew up in a very small family? Describe these families to a partner or to others in your class.

TALKING POINT

You can improve your understanding of things that you listen to if you have thought about the topic before you listen. For this reason, professors ask students to read about a lecture topic before class. Reading, talking with a partner, and brainstorming ideas about a topic on your own are all good ways to prepare for a difficult listening task.

Listen for Main Ideas

Listen to the interview with Jay Neugeboren, and answer these questions.

1. What is Neugeboren's definition of the word "family"?

    _____

2. List three or more words that describe Jay's family when he was a child.

    _____

3. List three or more words that describe the family in which Jay's children grew up.

    _____

Listen to Compare and Contrast

 How did Jay's family and childhood differ from his children's family and childhood? Write your answers in the following chart. Which type of family experience does Jay prefer? Why?

	Jay Neugeboren's Experience	His Children's Experience
Size of Immediate Family (mother, father, and siblings)		
Size of Extended Family (aunts, uncles, cousins, and so on)		
Location of Extended Family		

After You Listen

Compare your family and childhood to Jay Neugeboren's. Write your answers in the following chart. Which type of family experience do you prefer? Why?

	Your Experience	Jay Neugeboren's Experience
Size of Immediate Family (mother, father, and siblings)		
Size of Extended Family (aunts, uncles, cousins, and so on)		
Location of Extended Family		

Listening Two
Family: A Historical Viewpoint

The modern concept of family has changed, but how much? What were families like more than 300 years ago when North America was first being colonized by Europeans? To find out, we talked to Professor Carol Berkin, who teaches American Women's History at City University of New York.

Before You Listen

Look at this picture of a house that was built 300 years ago by some of the first Europeans to come to North America.

A typical home
300 years ago

Then, look at this picture of what some of the people who lived in this house might have looked like. Complete the chart that follows.

Actors dressed like a family
that lived in this home

How many people do you think lived in this home?	
Which family members would you guess lived here?	
What work did family members do?	
What do you think the lives of children were like in this home?	

Listen to Identify Key Terms

 Listen to the interview with Carol Berkin, and write the terms that she uses to identify each of the following concepts.

1. _____ was not valued by colonial people the way that it is today. People did not have their own rooms, and there was no assumption that you had to be all alone.

2. _____ was a term that colonial people used to refer to the skills that women had that turned the raw products of the farm into useful clothing and food.

3. _____ is one of the main reasons that Berkin thinks that the family has changed. Because families live in cities, people have been able to specialize and can buy many things that the farm produced.

4. _____ is the other reason that Berkin believes to have caused changes in families. Time-saving machinery means that we don't need large families to do work by hand.

5. _____ means that children are being supported by their families much longer than in the past. This has changed the relationship between parents and children and caused teenage rebellion and culture.

Listen for Details

Listen again to the interview with Carol Berkin to hear the answers to the following questions.

1. How often did a colonial woman have children?

    _____

2. In what room(s) did the children in a wealthy Southern planter's family live?

    _____

3. Who was the skilled worker in a colonial family? Who was the unskilled worker?

    _____

4. What are some of the skills that women had?

    _____

5. What was the size of the average colonial family?

    _____

6. What did John Deere invent?

    _____

7. By what age were eighteenth-century children "paying for themselves" by working on the farm?

    _____

After You Listen

How do families differ around the world? Choose a country or culture that you are familiar with or that you would like to study. Complete the following chart, and then share the information with others in your class.

How big is the typical family in this culture?	
Which family members usually live together?	
What work do family members do?	
What is a typical house like?	
How do children and teenagers live in this culture?	

NOTE
Taking

Basic Skills

In many cases when you listen, you must take notes to help you to remember what the speaker said. This is true in such situations as telephone calls, business meetings, and academic lectures. Taking good notes is not only a useful memory aid but also a way to improve your listening ability. The process of taking notes can help you to focus on important ideas and to listen to a speaker critically. As you work with this textbook, you will practice all of these skills.

There are many techniques and patterns that people use to organize notes. To help you to gain confidence and skill at taking notes, you will practice a variety of these techniques and patterns. You will then be able to choose the ones that work best for you.

Here are some general principles of note-taking.

1. Choose what you will include in your notes. As you listen, actively think about what you hear. Write only the important ideas and concepts.

2. Write phrases rather than sentences. It is impossible even for most native speakers of English to write down every word that a speaker says. If you try to write every word that you hear, your notes will probably contain only random phrases and will not help you to remember important ideas and concepts when you must study them later.

3. Try to make relationships between ideas clear in your notes. Use symbols, such as arrows, boxes, and stars, to highlight relationships and main ideas.

4. Use abbreviations when you take notes. You can use standard abbreviations such as these:

    | + (and) | = (equals, the same as) |
    | $ (dollars, money) | # (number) |
    | yr (year) | wk (week) |
    | U.S. (United States) | maj. (majority) |

    You also can use abbreviations that you create yourself, such as these:

    J.N. = Jay Neugeboren
    col. = colonial

5. Review your notes within six hours after you took them to write abbreviations out in complete words and to reinforce what you learned.

Example Notes

The following is an example of notes that a native speaker of English took while listening to the first part of the interview with Jay Neugeboren. Listen to the interview again, and follow along to see how the note-taking principles were followed.

Family is 2 people related
* by marriage → husband + wife
* mother + child
Also, extended family or small family
Bonded by blood, affection, relationship, long-term, responsible for
each other
Very different growing up around WWII than now
<u>*His family*</u>
Mother -- 1 of 8 children
Father -- 1 of 9 children
40 cousins

Listen again to the interview with Carol Berkin, and take notes. When you are finished, compare your notes with a partner's to see what information you might have missed.

Pronunciation ACTIVITIES

Thought Groups

Using complete thought groups is one of the most important things that you can do to improve the fluency of your spoken English. A *thought group* is a clause, phrase, or sentence that has a complete idea. The rules for what makes a thought group are much more flexible than are the rules for what makes a complete written sentence, and different speakers might divide the same sentence into slightly different thought groups. However, for most English speakers, the ends of grammatical clauses and phrases are also the ends of thought groups.

Examples:

clausal thought groups: Women had a skill …

So the extended childhood is very
          different …

phrasal thought groups: The average family …

As technology increased …

Complete thought groups are necessary to be understood for the following reasons.

- Speakers who use complete thought groups sound fluent, even when they speak slowly.
- Complete thought groups are less distracting than are thought groups broken by inappropriate pauses. They help listeners both to concentrate and to better understand the speaker's ideas.
- You need to use complete thought groups in order to use correct intonation and focal stress. (You will practice these pronunciation skills in later chapters.)

The first step toward making complete thought groups, and improving the fluency of your English, is to pause only at the end of a phrase, clause, and sentence.

Fluent-Sounding Examples:

If I were a parent / I think / I would want / a smaller family.
If I were a parent / I think I would want / a smaller family.

Disfluent-Sounding Example:

If I were a / parent I think / I would want a / smaller family.

You will learn more about the intonation and stress rules for thought groups in later chapters.

Listen for Thought Groups

In the following transcript of an excerpt from the interview with Carol Berkin, use slashes to mark the thought groups that she forms. The first few have been done for you. Then, discuss with a partner the questions that follow.

Most people lived on a farm, / and the farm was the economic production unit of the society, / and on that farm, / interestingly enough—and I love to tell my students this because they're so shocked—interestingly enough, the husband was the unskilled worker. He did the farming in the field. He produced the raw materials, and agricultural science was not very well developed. And so it was a pretty simple task all the way round. The mother, that is the housewife, engaged in something colonial people called "housewifery," which is not the same thing as housekeeping or housecleaning. Housewifery was a whole series of skilled processes, crafts that women employed and knew.

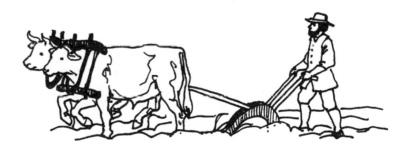

Discussion Questions

1. What kinds of grammatical structures are complete thought groups in this excerpt?

2. Locate any places where Berkin pauses in the middle of a thought group. What impression does it give you when this happens?

3. How might recognizing thought groups help you to be a more efficient listener? How can speaking in complete thought groups make you a more effective speaker?

Practice Speaking in Complete Thought Groups

Each of the following phrases can be the first complete thought group in a longer statement. Think about ways by which you could complete the statements, but do not write your answers before you speak. With a partner, take turns completing the statements with three or four thought groups, being sure to pause appropriately.

1. When I was a child …

2. The most important thing my family ever gave me …

3. I think growing up in a big family …

4. It's very important …

5. To me, the word family means …

Communicative Pronunciation Practice

Using thought groups and pauses well makes you sound more fluent and gives a listener a little bit more time to think about the ideas that you are expressing. To see how well you use thought groups, try the following activity.

1. Record yourself describing an interesting family or person whom you have met. If you take notes, write no more than ten words. Talk for about a minute but not much longer.

2. Listen to the tape, and write down every word that you said. This is called "making a transcript of the recording."

3. Read your transcript as you listen to the tape. Mark the thought groups that you made with double slashes. Circle any places at which you paused within a thought group.

4. With a different colored pen, mark the transcript with the thought groups and pauses that you think would be most effective.

5. Record yourself again. This time, read the transcript using the thought groups that you marked.

6. Compare the two recordings. What differences in comprehensibility do you notice?

7. For more practice, record your description a third time without using the transcript but focusing on using complete thought groups.

Additional Listening Practice with Thought Groups

An excellent way to practice hearing how speakers use thought groups is to listen to the thought groups used by radio and television news announcers when they read the news. Television news has fewer visual cues than do many other television shows, and there are no visual cues in radio programs. As a result, news announcers make a special effort to speak clearly in thought groups.

Watch or listen to such a news program, and then answer the following questions.

1. Can you easily hear the pitch falls and pauses that this newsperson uses to mark thought groups?

2. Do this newsperson's thought groups seem longer or shorter than those of people whom you talk to conversationally? What could be the reasons for these differences?

3. Are the main ideas of the news report easy to understand? How does the speaker make them clear?

TALK It Over!

Group Discussion

The ability to fully participate in a group discussion is important in a number of different areas. First, it is an important skill because college instructors often require this participation as a part of their coursework. Students are required to contribute their knowledge, experience, and information with others in the class. Second, in business, discussions are often a cornerstone of meetings. The ability to politely, yet firmly, express ideas and opinions can mean higher grades for students and promotions and raises for employees. In second-language courses, participation in discussions is an important tool for language learning.

Some language learners find participating in a discussion intimidating, whereas others might find that they are dominating the conversation so that others do not get a chance to talk. Use the following strategies to be sure that each discussion participant's ideas are included.

- When you want to speak, make eye contact with the person who is speaking or with the discussion leader. This not only lets this person know that you are interested in speaking, it also helps you to see when this person will finish speaking so that you can be ready to begin talking.
- Make a small polite noise just as someone finishes speaking. Saying "um" or "well" can let others know that you would like to speak. It also gives you a few extra seconds to think about what you want to say. However, after saying "um" or "well" don't wait too long to continue.
- Use body language. Lean forward or make a slight hand movement to signal that you want to speak.
- Speak in a voice strong enough to be heard clearly so that your group members can pay attention to what you are saying without making special effort.
- If you find that you are doing most of the talking, ask a question of someone who hasn't spoken and then wait for that person's response.

Prepare to Discuss

Think about the following questions. Make notes about your answers if you need to. Then share your answers with a small group of your classmates.

1. In your native language and culture, would a group discussion take place in a classroom? A club? A business meeting? In what other situations might a group discussion take place?

2. What do you do or say in your native language when you want to speak during a discussion?

Gather Ideas for a Discussion

One of the most important parts of a discussion is the preparation that you do before the discussion. Read any assignments carefully, and think about the discussion questions or topic.

In a part of the interview with Jay Neugeboren that you did not hear, he talks about some of the advantages of the smaller, more dispersed family in which his children grew up. Read his comments, and make notes of your answers to the questions that follow. Support your answers with details from the things that you have read and heard in this chapter.

Rob and I shared a very small room. When we opened a bed at night, you couldn't walk in the room. I mean it was that small. And there was very little privacy, and I think privacy is a wonderful thing. I think it's wonderful when you are growing up to feel that you have a place all your own, a place that's your own in your home for whatever you want to do in it. Whereas when I was growing up, and certainly I know my parents lived in very large families, there was little that was your own. So there's certainly advantages to a smaller family that way.

Probably there's some advantage to your cousins living far away because you get to see places you would never see otherwise. I never got west of New Jersey until I was twenty-one years old. Whereas my children, from an early age we would go and take trips to visit cousins and spend the weekend with them … . My parents moved to Florida when they retired, so we would visit them in Florida, so that my children have an experience very unlike mine. And yet I wouldn't put a weight on what's better or worse. I think they are different in quality.

Discussion Questions

1. How is your family and childhood different from or similar to your parents' families and childhoods? If you have or plan to have children, how will their experiences be different from yours?

2. Carol Berkin says that privacy was not valued in colonial times, and Jay Neugeboren says that "privacy is a wonderful thing." Is privacy something that you value highly? Can privacy ever be a bad thing?

3. Jay Neugeboren's children traveled to different places at young ages, but he did not. How far from home do you think colonial children got to travel? Is it important for children to see different places and to travel? How does travel affect your understanding of the world?

Participate in a Discussion

Use the notes that you prepared to discuss the questions on page 15. Before your discussion begins, choose one person in your group to perform each of the following duties. After the discussion, be prepared to report on your discussion to others in the class and use the evaluation form on page 147 to evaluate the discussion.

1. Group leader: Be sure that each person gets a chance to speak. Invite specific individuals to speak if they have not contributed. For example, ask them, "Have you had this experience?", "Do you agree with [Lin]?", or "I'd be interested to hear your reaction to that."

2. Note taker: Keep notes about the ideas discussed so that the discussion can be summarized for the class.

3. First speaker: Start the discussion by asking one of the questions or stating one of the ideas from your notes.

Further Practice

Living History Project

Interview an elderly or retired person about his or her family and childhood. This person may be an older member of your family or someone who lives in your community. Add at least three questions to the following list of possible interview questions. Choose five of these questions to ask the person. After the interview, report to your classmates about what you learned.

- How many people lived in your house when you were a child?
- What work did your parents do? How old were you when you first started working?
- What was being a teenager like? Did you rebel against your parents the way teenagers often do today?
- Did you travel much as a child? What places did you visit before you were an adult?

_____

_____

_____

_____

Agreeing and Disagreeing

Complete the following lists of phrases that you can use to politely agree and disagree with someone by adding two or more phrases to each list.

Phrases for Agreeing

I agree with you because …
That's exactly right …

_____

_____

_____

Phrases for Disagreeing

I don't think so …
That hasn't been my experience.
 I think …

_____

_____

_____

If you were discussing families with someone who made the following statements, would you agree or disagree? What would you say to each speaker to express your opinion?

1. I think even two friends who live together can be a family, if they care about each other a great deal and take care of each other.

2. I think that it's important for people to have big families. You learn a lot from brothers and sisters, and the more that you have, the better.

3. The most important reason to have children is so that they can take care of you when you get old.

4. Even families who live a long distance away from one another can be just as close as people who live in the same neighborhood as their grandparents or cousins.

Chapter 1: Self-Evaluation Chart

Use the following chart to record comments about your progress in mastering each of the following skills that you practiced in this chapter.

	+	–	Teacher's Comments
Note Taking • I understand this skill. • I am satisfied with my ability to use this skill. • I plan to use this skill again.			
Speaking Skills: Participating in a Discussion • I understand how to participate in a discussion. • I am satisfied with my ability to participate in a discussion.			
Pronunciation: Thought Groups • I understand what a thought group is. • I am satisfied with my ability to use thought groups in my speech. • I try to practice this skill in my everyday speaking.			

2
World
Entertainment

Brainstorming

Discuss your answers to the following questions with others in your class, or record your answers on tape. Consider magic acts, comedy, movies, cartoons, and any other types of entertainment that you can think of.

1. What kinds of entertainment do you think are universal and can be enjoyed by people from any culture?

2. What kinds of entertainment do not translate well from one culture to another?

Gathering Information from a Television Schedule

Find a prime-time (8 P.M.–11 P.M. or 7 P.M.–10 P.M.) weekday television schedule from a local newspaper or magazine, and use it to complete the following chart.

How many channels are listed? Choose ten major channels, and use the schedule to find the following information.	
How many of the **shows** are: game shows?	
news programs?	
situation comedies?	
educational programs?	
other types of programming?	
How many of the **movies** are: dramas?	
comedies?	
action?	
documentaries?	
horror?	
What kinds of rating systems or other information about the programs does the schedule provide for viewers?	

Use your answers in the preceding chart to discuss the following questions with others in your class.

1. What kinds of television entertainment are most popular on weeknights?

2. What other entertainment trends did you find in the television schedules? What reasons might explain these trends?

3. How are the prime-time viewing options in this area of the country similar to or different from programming in other places and countries with which you are familiar?

Listening One
The Universal Funny Bone

Before You Listen

In the following chart, indicate whether each type of entertainment is universal and can be enjoyed even by people who do not speak each other's languages. Explain why you made these choices.

Type of Entertainment	Can it be enjoyed universally?	Is knowledge of the language necessary to understand it?	Why?
Magic act			
Opera			
Comedy			
Drama			
Sports			
Radio talk show			
Pop music			
Other: _____			

Listen for the Main Idea

Listen to Jim O'Doherty, comedian and comedy writer, talk about "The Universal Funny Bone" to hear the answer to the following questions.

1. Does O'Doherty believe that there is any kind of humor that translates across languages and cultures?

   _____

2. If so, what is this "universal funny bone?"

   _____

Listen for Details

Listen to "The Universal Funny Bone" again, and choose the best answer to these questions.

1. Which of these statements is not true?

   a. Different cultures think different things are funny.

   b. One group could be offended by something that another group finds funny.

   c. A person's sense of humor is affected very little by his or her culture.

   d. Both a and b.

2. What did the audience find funny about this comedian's encounter with the Asian businessman?

   a. The businessmen were laughing hysterically.

   b. The repeated bowing.

   c. Americans look funny when they try to bow.

   d. There was no English spoken, but they still communicated.

3. In the story about bowing, who bowed first?

   a. The Asian businessman.

   b. Jim O'Doherty.

   c. The liaison for the group of Asian businessmen.

   d. They all bowed at the same time.

4. What was funny about the act that the comedian performed in which he produced a dove from colored scarves?

   a.   He killed the bird by clapping his hands.

   b.   The bird was very beautiful.

   c.   People were fooled into believing that the bird was real.

   d.   The audience had a funny reaction.

5. What does the term "funny bone" mean in this talk?

   a.   Physical humor.

   b.   An unusual bone in the human body.

   c.   A place where a person laughs when tickled.

   d.   Sense of humor.

After You Listen

With a partner, retell O'Doherty's stories about times when he was able to make people laugh without using any English. One person should tell the first story, and the other should tell the second story.

Just for Fun!

Write down a funny saying from a bumper sticker or button that you have seen, or find a funny cartoon. Take either with you to class. In a small group, examine the words and pictures and answer the following questions.

1. Why is this bumper sticker, button, or cartoon funny? What is the joke?

2. Do you need any special cultural knowledge to "get" this joke?

3. What kind of person would probably find this joke to be funny? What kind of person might think the joke is not very funny?

Listening Two
Game Shows Go Global

Before You Listen

Discuss the following questions with a group of your classmates.

1. Do you like to watch game shows? Why or why not?

2. Describe a game show that you know about. With your group, list the similarities and differences among the shows that are described.

3. Do you think that there is any kind of game show that is popular worldwide? Why or why not?

Listen for Main Ideas

 In this interview, Anne Cooper-Chen, a journalism professor, identifies four patterns that she found when she researched game shows around the world. As you listen to the interview, label the following map to show where each pattern is usually found.

Listen for Details

 Listen to the interview again to hear the answers to the following questions. If you need to, listen more than once.

1. Why does almost every country have a game show?

   _____

2. Did Anne Cooper-Chen have difficulty understanding the game shows that she studied? Why or why not?

   _____

3. Write three characteristics of each of the four game show patterns.

   Western Pattern   Latin American Pattern

   a.   a.
   b.   b.
   c.   c.

   Asian Pattern   Equatorial/Educational Pattern

   a.   a.
   b.   b.
   c.   c.

4. What does Anne Cooper-Chen think can be learned from her research on game shows around the world?

   _____

5. What kinds of prizes do contestants receive on game shows?

   _____

NOTE Taking

Listing

One way to take notes while you are listening is to list related information under a single main idea. Sometimes you will hear the main idea first, and sometimes you will learn the main idea after you have listed the details. If you do not hear the main idea immediately, leave space in your notes to add it later. When you identify a main idea, underline it.

 The following is an example of notes that a native speaker of English took while listening to the first part of the talk by Jim O'Doherty. Listen to the interview again, and follow along to see how these note-taking principles were followed.

Universal Funny Bone
<u>Diff Cultures = diff sensibilities</u>
-- smthg can be demeaning to one
-- can be hilarious to another
<u>1st Ex.: Asian Businessmen</u>
-- Jim wanted to welcome them
-- when introduced, Jim bowed
-- Bus. man bowed back
-- Jim bowed again
-- reflex: Jim understood if he bowed, man would bow
-- everyone thought it was funny but no language used

 Listen again to the interview with Anne Cooper-Chen, and complete the following notes. Write important details in note form under the main ideas. If necessary, you may listen more than once.

Which Countries Have Game Shows	Language Was Not a Problem
Almost every country	_____
small studio, camera, host	_____
contestants -- free	_____
Any country can do game	_____
shows cheaply	_____

Western Pattern	Asian Pattern
_____	_____
_____	_____
_____	_____
_____	_____

Latin American Pattern	Equatorial/Educational Pattern
_____	_____
_____	_____
_____	_____
_____	_____

Prizes	Who Loves Game Shows the Most
_____	_____
_____	_____
_____	_____
_____	_____

After You Listen

Relating What You Hear to Personal Experience

Use the notes that you took while listening to the interview with Anne Cooper-Chen to help you to think about your own experiences with game shows and to answer the following questions. Share your answers with a small group, and then summarize your discussion for others in your class.

TALKING POINT

> The information that you hear is more memorable when you take time after listening to relate the ideas that you heard to your personal experiences, knowledge, and opinions.

1. What countries' game shows have you seen? What patterns are common in these countries? Do the patterns that you have experienced match the pattern that Anne Cooper-Chen's research predicts?

2. If possible, think of a game show that you have seen that matches each pattern. (Write the game shows' names in the original language, and translate them into English if you can.)

3. Anne Cooper-Chen gives some reasons why she thinks some game shows are popular in some countries. Do you agree or disagree with the reasons that she gives?

4. Anne Cooper-Chen says, "There is no one type of entertainment that seems to be right for all cultures." Do you agree or disagree? Do you find television programs in your own country and other countries to be equally entertaining?

5. Have you ever watched U.S. television shows in another country? Why do you think that these shows become popular there?

Pronunciation ACTIVITIES

Intonation in Questions and Statements

Intonation is one of the most important ways that English speakers express meaning. In fact, it can be just as important to use correct intonation as it is to use the correct grammar for a question. In this chapter, you will study the intonation patterns for making statements and answering questions.

A steep rise in pitch can indicate that a speaker is unsure about something, so questions will usually have high, rising intonation. Falling intonation communicates the feeling that the speaker is sure about what is being said, so it is used when making statements. There are three basic patterns.

1. **Yes/No Questions:**   In yes/no questions, the focal word of the question has a slight drop in pitch followed by a steeper rise in pitch. The rise in pitch continues to the end of the question.

   Example: Do you avoid television shows with lots of violence?

2. *Wh–* **Questions:**   In *Wh–* questions, which use the words "who," "what," "when," "where," "why," and "how," the intonation rises and then falls on the focal word of the question and then continues to fall until the end of the thought group.

   Example: What kind of movies do you like?

3. **Statements:**   In statements, the intonation falls at the end of the statement.

   Example: I enjoy watching documentary programs.

Predict Intonation in Questions and Statements

Predict where the intonation should rise and fall in the following questions and statements from the interview with Anne Cooper-Chen. Add the correct punctuation to each sentence, and draw arrows to show your predictions.

1. Are TV game shows popular in other parts of the world

2. Do many countries have game shows

3. Just about every country has a game show

4. How did you study the game shows

5. Weren't they in all different languages

6. They're very cheap to produce, and there's a high profit margin

7. They have more game shows than any other country in the world

8. What did you learn from watching all the global TV

9. There's no one type of entertainment that seems to be right for all cultures

10. Who loves game shows the most

Practice Intonation in Questions and Statements

 Now listen to those same questions and statements. Draw arrows to show the intonation that you actually hear. Finally, repeat after the speaker, pronouncing the intonation as the speaker does.

1. Are TV game shows popular in other parts of the world

2. Do many countries have game shows

3. Just about every country has a game show

4. How did you study the game shows

5. Weren't they in all different languages

6. They're very cheap to produce, and there's a high profit margin

7. They have more game shows than any other country in the world

8. What did you learn from watching all the global TV

9. There's no one type of entertainment that seems to be right for all cultures

10. Who loves game shows the most

Practice Listening

For more practice hearing question intonation patterns, you can watch a game show and pay special attention to the intonation patterns used when the host asks questions and when the contestant answers. Interview programs and talk shows are also a rich source of questions and answers.

Communicative Pronunciation Practice

Interview your classmates about the things that they do for entertainment.

1. Brainstorm a list of five questions that you could ask your classmates to find out what kinds of entertainment they like and why. Try to think of original questions, and use a mixture of yes/no questions and *Wh–* questions.

    Examples: Do you usually understand comedy and jokes in English?
                    What do you like to do to relax on the weekends?

    _____

    _____

    _____

    _____

    _____

2. Choose three questions from your list that you will ask. Mark the intonation pattern on the questions, and practice asking the questions with the correct intonation.

3. Circulate in the class, and ask three or more of your classmates these questions and answer their questions.

4. Share some of the interesting things that you learned with others in the class. Tell them your questions and the answers that you received.

TALK It Over!

Asking and Answering Questions

Often in game shows, contestants must ask or answer questions. Usually on a game show, the rules of the game dictate who asks questions and how and when the questions must be answered. In conversations, classrooms, and business interactions, there also are some rules that are followed when people ask and answer questions, but the rules are rarely explained clearly as they are on a game show.

Answering Questions

When you are answering a question, use the following strategies to keep your conversation going smoothly.

- Begin to answer the question within three seconds. If you wait longer than three seconds to answer, the person who asked the question might assume that you didn't understand or think that you don't want to answer the question.

- If you need time to answer the question, make a sound or gesture that lets the person who asked the question know that you intend to answer. You can say "hmm," nod your head, or, while you think, say "Let me think about that" or "That's a tough question to answer."

- If you don't understand the question, you can say, "Do you mean …" and ask the question in your own words, or you can ask the person who asked the question to restate or rephrase the question.

- After you answer the question, you can make sure that your listeners understood your answer by saying, "Do you know what I mean?" or "Is that clear?"

Practice Answering Questions

Play a question answering game with a group of your classmates.

1. Before you begin, prepare the questions. Each classmate can write several questions to ask or use questions from a trivia game or book.

2. Write the question on one side of a piece of paper, and write the answer on the other side of the paper. Be sure to ask questions that your classmates will be able to answer.

3. Divide your class or group into two teams.

4. The first team asks one of its questions. The second team tries to answer the question correctly. Then the second team asks a question for the first team to answer. If you would like, you can keep score.

5. As you play, practice using correct intonation patterns as well as the strategies for answering questions.

Asking Questions

If you are answering a question in a conversation, you can keep the conversation going by ending your answer with a question for the people to whom you are speaking. Use the following tips to help you to ask appropriate questions.

- Think about the type of answer that you would like to receive. If you want a very specific answer, be sure that you ask a very specific question. If you want the person with whom you are speaking to give you a longer answer, ask an open-ended question using a word or phrase such as "why," "how," and "tell me about …"
- Remember to assess the appropriateness of the question. Questions about money, personal relationships, and physical attributes (such as weight and age) are usually not appropriate except among close friends in informal situations.
- If you know that you will have to ask questions in a formal situation, such as a survey or an interview, you can plan some of the questions ahead of time. However, if an answer needs clarification or contains interesting information that you would like to know more about, you should ask by saying, "Interesting. But could you tell me more about …" or "Could you explain what you mean by …" You will get the information that you want, and your conversation will be more natural for you and the person to whom you are speaking.
- Review English question intonation and word order, and practice your questions until it is natural for you to use intonation correctly.

Practice Answering Questions

Interview someone who is not a member of your class about the kind of entertainment that this person enjoys. Follow these steps.

1. Decide about what type of entertainment you will ask questions. Some possibilities are movies, television, music, and theater.

2. Write at least five questions that you will ask in the interview. Show these questions to a partner, who will help you to revise your questions and choose four questions to ask.

3. Introduce yourself, and ask the person whom you plan to interview for permission to conduct the interview.

4. Record or take notes about the person's answers to your questions.

5. Be prepared to share the responses that you received with others in your class.

Useful Expressions

Use the following expressions when you do your interview.
To start the interview:

- "Hello, my name is …, and I am doing a project for my English class. Would you mind if I ask you a few questions about the kind of entertainment that you enjoy?"

If the person whom you ask would rather not answer the questions or doesn't have time to talk:

- "Thank you anyway."
- "OK. Thank you for your time."

When you need more time to make a note of the person's answer:

- "Just a second. I want to write that down."
- "Could you repeat the last part so I can make a note of it?"

When you would like the person whom you are interviewing to elaborate on what was said:

- "Tell me more about …"
- "That's really interesting. Could you elaborate on that?"

Further Practice

Game Shows on the Internet

For more information about these (and other game shows), check out their sites on the Internet. Some Internet sites explain how you can be a contestant, give the history of the show, let you play the game online, and more. Some people who have been contestants have put up World Wide Web sites about their experiences. You can find these and other shows' sites by typing the show's name into any Web directory or search engine.

Wheel of Fortune   http://www.station.sony.com/wheel/
Jeopardy   http://jeopardy.station.sony.com
The Price Is Right   http://www.cbs.com/daytime/price
Who Wants to Be a Millionaire?   http://abc.go.com/primetime/
     millionaire/millionaire_home.html

Listening in the Real World

Watching a Television Game Show

Watch a television game show, and try to analyze the show the same way Anne Cooper-Chen analyzed game shows in her book. As you watch the show, answer the following questions.

1. When is the show on television? _____

2. Who are the contestants, and how are they chosen?

   _____

3. How does a contestant win the game?

   _____

4. What kinds of prizes do the contestants win?

   _____

5. From the content and format of the game show, what can you tell about the intended audience of the show? For example, what are their ages and economic or educational levels?

   _____

6. Which one of the patterns identified by Anne Cooper-Chen does the show follow?

   _____

Compare your answers with a group of classmates. Choose one show that your group will describe to others in your class.

Chapter 2: Self-Evaluation Chart

Use the following chart to record comments about your progress in mastering each of the following skills that you practiced in this chapter.

	+	−	Teacher's Comments
Note Taking: Listing • I understand this skill. • I am satisfied with my ability to use this skill. • I plan to use this skill again.			
Speaking Skills: Asking and Answering Questions • I understand the tips for asking and answering questions. • I am satisfied with my ability to use these tips. • I plan to use them in the future by _____ .			
Pronunciation: Intonation — Questions and Statements • I understand the importance of this use of intonation. • I am satisfied with my ability to use this concept. • I try to practice this in my everyday speaking.			

3

Environmental Activism

Listening	Note Taking	Pronunciation	Speaking
Inference Time order Main ideas	Cause and effect organizational patterns	Syllable stress in compound words and phrasal verbs	Defending an opinion

Brainstorming

Discuss your answers to the following questions with others in your class, or record your answers on tape.

1. What concerns, if any, do you have about environmental problems?

2. What actions have you, or could you have, taken to protect the environment?

Gathering Information from a Reading

Read the following passage about environmental activism in different countries. Then, with others in your class, discuss the questions that follow it.

Environmental Problem Solving

Over the last fifty years, there has been growing concern about keeping our living environment clean and livable. This concern has taken a variety of forms both within and across cultures. Because of economic, social, cultural, and environmental factors, however, there are trends as to the types of problems that environmental groups focus on and the types of activism in which they engage.

One of the most widely known environmental activist groups is Greenpeace. Greenpeace International's Web site (www.greenpeace.com) lists a number of environmental issues about which this organization is concerned, including global warming, toxic waste, nuclear waste, ocean pollution, genetic engineering, and deforestation. There are many other organizations in addition to Greenpeace, and they are often called NGOs, which stands for Nongovernmental Organizations. People who work and volunteer for these organizations try to influence the political process in order to protect the environment.

Another kind of activism is "grassroots" environmental activism. *Grassroots* means that people work together at a local level to solve a problem. Usually grassroots organizations spread information about the problem and try to build the number of people who are concerned about the issue so that political leaders cannot ignore the problem. In the *Electronic Green Journal*, Laurie Kutner, with the University of Vermont, reports that the first grassroots organizations focused on issues of conserving wilderness areas and protecting wildlife. Now, however, from 7,000 to 8,000 grassroots organizations are working to have toxic waste removed from their communities or to prevent it from being brought into the areas in which they live.[1]

Both NGOs and grassroots organizations work hard to influence government officials to make decisions that will protect the environment. They encourage people to write letters to government leaders, have meetings with government leaders to advance their causes, and even run for political office. The Green Party has been influential in Europe for some time and has typically been less powerful in the United States. In 2000, however, the Green Party candidate for U.S. president got enough votes that his candidacy might have influenced the outcome of the election, although not in the way that environmentalists had hoped.

Finally, people are able to work for environmental change on an individual level. Reducing the amount of products and resources that we consume, making the effort to conserve resources, and using products made from recycled paper and plastic are all ways that individuals can have an impact. The Internet also provides ways for people to find information about the environment, contact political leaders using email, and even post their own Web pages that support the environmental causes important to them. A quick search of Web sites shows a number of pages posted by individuals from Russia to Peru on topics as varied as preventing pollution in the Barents Sea to providing sustainable occupations for the native women who live in the rainforests of South America.

Discussion Questions

1. In many countries, there is a lot of tension between industry and environmental activists. Do you think that it is more important for a government to make laws that develop industry or that protect the environment? Is it possible to do both?

2. Should the government or industry be responsible for solving environmental problems? In what ways, if any, can individuals solve environmental problems?

3. The previous article mentions two ways by which people try to solve problems: politically and through grassroots volunteer organizations. What do you think are the strengths of each of these methods? What are their weaknesses? What are other methods of problem solving?

Listening One
Wildlife Survival

Before You Listen

Discuss the following questions with a group of your classmates.

1. What is an *endangered species*? Make a list of five animals that you believe are on the endangered species list.

2. Look at the following photograph, and list five ideas that the word "wolf" makes you think of.

The Big Bad Wolf _____   _____

_____   _____

_____   _____

3. Why might people be nervous about having wolves live near their homes?

Listen for Inference

An *inference* is a guess that you make based on information that you have been given. Listen to Suzanne Laferty talk about her work helping to restore wolves to their natural habitat in Idaho and infer the answers to the following questions. If necessary, you may listen several times.

1. For how long has the effort to restore wolves been occurring?

   _____

2. How did the activists change people's attitudes toward the wolf?

   _____

3. Does this activist believe that wolves are now fully recovered? How do you know?

   _____

Listen for Time Order

The following time line lists some of the important dates and time periods that Laferty mentions in the process of restoring wolves to their natural habitat in Idaho. As you listen to her talk about wolves, fill in the events that took place, are taking place, or will take place at these times. There sometimes will be more than one event at a certain date or during a given time period.

⟵──⟶

End of the 1960s   1973   Ten years ago   Now   The Future

After You Listen

With a partner or on tape, use the information in the time line to retell Suzanne Laferty's story about saving the wolves.

Listening Two
The Road to Mt. Dioxin

Before You Listen

Think about the following questions, and write notes for your answers.
Then discuss your answers with others in your class.

1. What would you do if you found out that a factory in your community
   was causing pollution?

2. What if the pollution from the factory was
   a. harming an endangered species?
   b. endangering human health?

Listen for Main Ideas

Listen to this report about Margaret Williams, an activist working to get
toxic waste cleaned up in her community. As you listen, note the answers to
the following questions.

1. What is the problem in Pensacola, Florida?

   _____

2. What have members of the community done to try to solve this
   problem?

   _____

3. Has the problem been solved?

   _____

<table>
<tr><td>

NOTE
Taking

</td><td>

Cause and Effect Organizational Patterns

In this documentary about Margaret Williams's activism to clean up polluted soil in Pensacola, Florida, she discusses the causes and effects of the pollution in her community. Listening for organizational patterns such as causes and effects can help you to select what to write in your notes.

One way to make notes of causes and effects is to do so in columns. Another is to use symbols such as arrows to illustrate the relationships between causes and effects.

</td></tr>
</table>

 The following is an example of notes that a native speaker of English took while listening to the first part of the talk by Suzanne Laferty. Listen to the interview again, and follow along to see how these note-taking principles were followed.

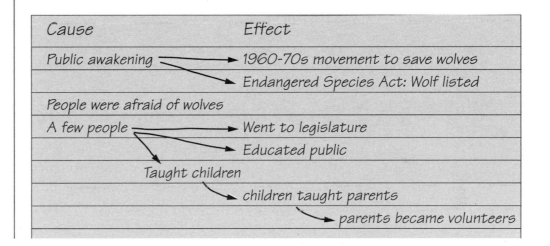

Cause	Effect
Public awakening	1960-70s movement to save wolves
	Endangered Species Act: Wolf listed
People were afraid of wolves	
A few people	Went to legislature
	Educated public
Taught children	
	children taught parents
	parents became volunteers

 Listen again to the documentary with Margaret Williams, and take notes about the causes and effects that are discussed. Use arrows, columns, or both as strategies for organizing your notes.

After You Listen

Compare Suzanne Laferty's story of restoring the wolves in Idaho with Margaret Williams's story. Use your notes to answer the following questions.

1. Approximately how long have activists been working to solve the environmental problem in each area?

   _____

2. What has each group of activists done that is similar? What has each done that is different?

   _____

3. List three suggestions that Suzanne Laferty might give Margaret Williams and Citizens Against Toxic Exposure to help solve their environmental problem.

   _____

Pronunciation ACTIVITIES

Syllable Stress in Compound Words and Phrasal Verbs

You have probably learned that every English word has at least one stressed syllable that is longer, louder, and higher-pitched that any other syllable in the word. If you stress the incorrect syllable, listeners might misunderstand the word or even the whole phrase in which it is found.

In English, a syllable can be stressed one of three ways.

1. One syllable in the word will have the strongest stress, called *primary stress.* In this textbook, regular capital letters mark PRIMARY STRESS.

2. Sometimes a syllable is stressed but not as strongly as the primary stress syllable. This is called *secondary stress,* marked in this textbook in small capital letters: SECONDARY STRESS.

3. Some syllables are unstressed. These syllables often have reduced vowels and are marked with lowercase letters: unstressed.

There are many rules for syllable stress, and while it is not practical to memorize every rule, learning the following can help you better understand the stress patterns of English.

• A *compound noun* is usually stressed on the stressed syllable of the first noun in the pair.

   Examples: comMUNity GROUP, GRANDFATHer

- An *adjective/noun pair* usually has primary stress on the second word in the pair.

  Examples: The WHITE house is at 1600 Pennsylvania Avenue in Washington, D.C.
  The white HOUSE on our street needs to be painted.

- A *compound verb* is usually stressed on the primary-stressed syllable of the second word that makes up the compound.

  Examples: outLAST, overRUN

- A *three-word compound word* is usually stressed on the first word of the two most closely related words in the pair. If a three-word compound word includes an adjective, the noun always receives primary stress.

  Examples: CHEMical WOOD preservatives, SERious HEALTH PRoblems

- A *number* is usually stressed on the first syllable. There are a couple of exceptions.
  A number that ends in "–teen" is stressed on the last syllable.

  Examples: SEvenTEEN (not SEVenty), fourTEEN (not FOURty)

  When a hyphenated number comes at the end of a thought group, the primary stress moves to the last syllable.

  Examples: They earned TWENty-FIVE dollars a week.
  On my birthday, I'll be TWENty-FIVE.

- In most *phrasal verbs* (two-word verbs), the first word receives primary stress but the preposition receives secondary stress. Prepositions that are not part of phrasal verbs are usually unstressed.

  Examples: HANDed OUT, GO ON, CLEAN UP
  we WALKed in the GARden.

Practice Syllable Stress in Compound Words and Phrasal Verbs

 Listen to the following compound words and phrasal verbs from the documentary on Mt. Dioxin. Underline syllables with primary stress twice, and underline syllables with secondary stress once.

1. telephone poles
2. working class
3. African-American neighborhood
4. look back
5. twenty-five dollars

6. environmental group
7. covered up
8. seven million dollars
9. hazardous waste landfills
10. go through with

Listen again, and repeat each item after the speaker. Be sure to pronounce the syllable stress as the speaker does.

Practice Syllable Stress in Compound Words and Phrasal Verbs

Student A: Check one question in each of the following pairs. Do not tell Student B which question you checked. Read it to Student B.

Student B: Listen to the question that Student A reads. Check the appropriate ending from column two of the following list.

After you both have completed all of the items, compare your answers. Then, reverse roles and repeat the exercise.

Column One

1. ____ Do you have a BLACK BELT
   ____ Do you have a BLACK belt

2. ____ Can you hear the LOUD SPEAKer

   ____ Can you hear the LOUDSPEAKer

3. ____ Did she get a GREEN CARD
   ____ Did she get a GREEN card

Column Two

____ to match these shoes?
____ in martial arts?

____ on my car's stereo system?
____ announcement?

____ or a blue one?
____ before her visa expired?

4. ____ Do you need a DARK ROOM   ____ to sleep in, or do you
                                                 like to have a light?

    ____ Do you need a DARKroom   ____ to develop the
                                                 photographs?

5. ____ What is the FIRST NAME   ____ on the list of
                                                 students?

    ____ What is the FIRST NAME   ____ and last name of the
                                                 winner?

6. ____ Was the RIGHT WING   ____ of the bird injured?
    ____ Was the RIGHT WING   ____ of the political party
                                                 the most conservative?

Communicative Pronunciation Practice

To practice using word stress correctly, record a summary of the documentary about Mt. Dioxin. Use notes, and do not read a written paragraph word for word. Follow these steps.

1. Make a list of the most important ideas and concepts that you heard about in this documentary. For example, you could write "Many health problems—caused by factories" instead of "Today, people are suffering from many health problems caused by two factories in their town."

2. Rewrite the list, and underline the main ideas. Number them in the order in which you plan to present them.

3. Mark the correct syllable stress on the multi-syllable words in your notes.

4. Using your notes, practice your oral summary. Pay particular attention to stressing the words correctly.

5. Record your summary.

TALKING POINT

Recording yourself is a great way to practice your pronunciation. You can listen to yourself and train your ear to hear your mistakes. Make a note of any words that you stressed incorrectly, and rerecord the words with the correct stress.

Defending an Opinion

Activists are frequently required to express their opinions to many people —government leaders, corporate officials, and other people whose opinions differ from the activists' opinions. You will probably often be called upon to express your opinions on a variety of issues. In debating, the ability to defend your opinion is critical to the success of the argument.

Tips to Help You Defend Your Opinions

1. Know what your opinion is, and state it clearly. You can use an expert's opinion to support your own. Use phrases such as "As Margaret Williams explained …" or "Like Suzanne Laferty, I, too, believe …"

2. Provide support for your opinion. Use facts or personal experience to support your opinion, and make sure that the facts relate directly to your opinion. Use phrases such as "A recent study concluded …" or "The best example of this is …" Never knowingly give false information to support your opinion.

3. It is especially important to think of the questions that someone with a different opinion might ask you so that you can plan responses to those questions.

Practice Defending Your Opinion

To help you practice defending your opinions, hold a debate with your classmates. Follow these steps.

1. Brainstorm a list of five topics that could be debated in class. Phrase the topics as yes/no questions.

    Examples: Should wilderness areas be protected from development, no matter what the cost to business and economic opportunities?
    Should the government pass very strict laws to reduce the pollution caused by cars?

2. Form groups of four to six students. Within each group, form two teams of two to three students who will work together to defend the team's opinion. One team will answer "yes" to the question; the other team will answer "no." As you form teams and choose the question that you will debate, remember that it is excellent speaking practice to

try to defend an opinion that is different from your own. (If you can learn to defend opinions that you disagree with, it will be easy to defend opinions that you believe are valid!)

3. Work with your team to collect facts, examples, and personal anecdotes to defend your team's opinion. Check the library or the Internet for information, if necessary.

4. Decide how much time you can devote to the debate to determine the speaking times for the debate. For example, if you will do several debates in front of the class, the speaking times must be shorter than if you do several debates at once in groups. Fill in the time limits in the spaces in step 5.

5. Use the following pattern when you debate.

The Yes team presents its opinion.   (Time limit: _____ minutes)

The No team presents its opinion.   (Time limit: _____ minutes)

The Yes team asks the No team questions. (Time limit: _____ minutes)

The No team asks the Yes team questions. (Time limit: _____ minutes)

The Yes team summarizes its opinion,   (Time limit: _____ minutes)
including answers to the questions asked by the No team.

The No team summarizes its opinion,   (Time limit: _____ minutes)
including answers to the questions asked by the Yes team.

TALKING POINT

Your opinion will be more respected by the audience if you support it with clearly explained reasons and facts.

Further Practice

Listening to a Television or Radio Documentary

A *documentary* is a television or radio program that gives in-depth, accurate information on one subject. It is common for documentaries to be about wildlife, history, famous people, countries, current events, and other topics. Find out which television or radio stations in your area often present documentary programs, watch or listen to one of these programs, and then answer the following questions.

Title of program: _____

Television or radio channel that broadcasted it: _____

Date/time of program: _____

What is the main theme of this documentary? _____

_____

Write three interesting facts that you learned from this documentary.

_____

_____

_____

Give a brief summary of the program that you watched to others in your class.

Community Activism

Community problems are almost never decided quickly and easily. Many people's opinions must be heard and considered, and often compromises much be reached. Usually even a group that wins the first vote continues to meet because they know that the group that did not win will try to push its issue again, in a new way. The following are the steps that activists employ when trying to solve a community problem.

1. Conduct research to identify the following.
   - Who are the individuals, government officials, and companies involved?
   - What financial conditions affect the problem?
   - What are possible solutions to the problem?

2. Meet with others who are concerned about the problem to plan a strategy.

3. Make a list of steps that the group must take.
   - Meet with officials.
   - Write letters.
   - Publicize the group's position, and make others aware of the problem.

4. Decide who will complete each task and how it will be done.

5. Set the time and place for the next meeting.

Find out about an issue on your campus or in your community. Work with a group of classmates to determine one thing that you might do to solve this problem.

Chapter 3: Self-Evaluation Chart

Use the following chart to record comments about your progress in mastering each of the following skills that you practiced in this chapter.

	+	–	Teacher's Comments
Note Taking: Cause and Effect • I understand these skills. • I am satisfied with my ability to use these skills. • I plan to use these skills again.			
Speaking Skills: Defending an Opinion • I understand how to defend my opinion. • I am satisfied with my ability to defend my opinion.			
Pronunciation: Syllable Stress in Compound Words and Phrasal Verbs • I understand how to use syllable stress in compound words and phrasal verbs. • I am satisfied with my ability to use syllable stress. • I try to practice this in my everyday speaking.			

4

The Sounds
of Language

Brainstorming

Discuss your answers to the following questions with others in your class, or record your answers on tape.

Have you ever tried to change your accent? Why? What were the results?

Accents and Dialects

In a group, discuss how you would define the following words:

a. accent

b. dialect

Now, read the following text to learn the difference between the words "accent" and "dialect."

The Difference Between Accents and Dialects

The meanings of the words "accent" and "dialect" are somewhat similar, and some people use them as if they mean the same thing. So, what is the difference between an accent and a dialect? An *accent* is the sounds and rhythms with which a person speaks a language. A *dialect* is more than sounds and rhythms. It includes the vocabulary and grammar used in a specific region or by a specific group of people, as well as the sounds and rhythms with which those people speak. Therefore, an accent can be part of a dialect, but a dialect is more than just an accent.

Finally, it is important to note that everyone has an accent in every language spoken. This accent might be a standard mainstream accent, a regional accent, or a foreign accent, but everyone has one.

Discuss the following questions with a group of your classmates.

1. How do the previous explanations of the words "accent" and "dialect" compare to the definitions that you decided on in your group?

2. What dialects can you recognize in the languages that you speak? Is one dialect of this language considered more desirable than others?

3. If you could choose to speak English with any kind of accent, which would you choose? Why?

Listening One
A Taste of French

Before You Listen

Think about the following discussion questions. Talk about the answers with a group of your classmates.

1. Describe an experience in which your accent was helpful or harmful to you in some way.

2. Is it always necessary for a person to try to get rid of a foreign or regional accent? When might an accent be desirable?

3. How do you think a person's identity and accent might be related?

Listen to Understand Attitudes

You will hear Carol Paradis, a French chef who teaches French cooking. He explains why he likes his French accent.

Listen to Carol Paradis speak to hear the answers to the following questions.

1. How did the chef feel about his French accent when he was younger?

   _____

2. How has his attitude toward his own accent changed?

   _____

3. Why has his attitude about his accent changed now that he is an adult?

   _____

Listen for Details

Listen again to hear the answers to the following questions.

1. Why did the chef want to change his accent when he was younger?
    How did he try to make these changes?

    _____

    _____

2. Make a list of three reasons why the chef thinks that it is important for
    him to have a French accent now.

    _____

    _____

3. Why do people expect a French chef to have a French accent?

    _____

    _____

4. What effect did Carol Paradis's accent have on his student from
    New York?

    _____

    _____

After You Listen

Discuss the following questions with a group of your classmates.

Do you feel that it is important for you to try to change your accent?
Why or why not? Which of the following reasons are good reasons for trying
to change the way in which you speak? Why?

1. I want other people to understand me.

2. I want to fit in so that people do not treat me like an outsider.

3. I want to speak the language like a native.

4. When I do something, such as learn a language, I like to do it right.

Listening Two
The Dialect Coach

Think about the following questions, and note your answers for each. Discuss your answers with a group of your classmates.

1. What movies have you watched in which an actor has learned a new accent in order to play his or her character? What accents can you identify in these movies?

2. What techniques do you think actors use to try to change their accents for certain roles?

3. Do the accents of the actors ever make it difficult for you to understand a movie? What helps you to understand an accent?

Listen for Main Ideas

Jessica Drake is one of Hollywood's top dialect coaches. Her job is to help actors add or remove accents according to the requirements of the movie or television show. She has worked with actors such as Tom Hanks, Russell Crowe, Angela Bassett, and Johnny Depp. She has reduced Swedish accents and created Cajun ones. Drake explains how she does her job.

 Read the following list of topics. As you listen to the interview for the first time, mark an X on the line next to the ideas that Jessica Drake talks about. Then, compare your answers with those of a partner.

____ The process of teaching an actor to use an accent

____ Designing a dialect for the movie *Forrest Gump*

____ Why there are many different accents spoken in the American South

____ How a character in a film and an accent develop together

____ How Forrest Gump's dialect sounded

____ The accent used by other characters in *Forrest Gump*

____ How long it takes an actor to learn a dialect

____ Funny stories about actors learning dialects

____ The effect that an accent has on an actor's body language

____ Qualities that a good dialect coach must have

NOTE
Taking

The Cornell Method

The Cornell method of note taking was developed at Cornell University. To use this method of note taking, draw a line about one-third of the distance from the left edge of a piece of paper. (See the following example.) Take notes on the right side of the line. On the left side of the line, write main ideas, important words, terms being defined, and questions answered in the body of the notes. You can save time and be more accurate by filling in the left side of the paper after you have finished taking notes.

 The following is an example of notes that a native speaker of English took while listening to the first part of the talk by Carol Paradis. Listen to the interview again, and follow along to see how these note-taking principles have been followed.

Accent is asset	
	-- people trust you esp. if teaching French cuisine
When younger	
	-- he thought he had bad Eng. bec. of accent
	-- practiced in front of TV: Flintstones, Johnny Carson
	-- practiced w/ mirror way of moving mouth

 Listen again to the interview with Jessica Drake, and take notes by using the Cornell method of note taking. Then, use your notes to answer the questions on the next page.

1. Briefly explain the process that Jessica Drake follows to teach someone a dialect.

    _____

    _____

2. In what American dialects is pin/pen inversion commonly found?

    _____

3. Name one of the unique or unusual things about the accent that Tom Hanks used for the character Forrest Gump.

    _____

4. Does an accent affect body language?

    _____

5. What does Jessica Drake believe are the requirements for being a good dialect coach?

    _____

After You Listen

Consider how the information that you just heard about accents in film applies to you as a student of English. Discuss the following questions with a small group of your classmates.

1. What is similar about an actor learning a dialect and a student of English changing a foreign accent? What is different about these two situations?

2. Jessica Drake talks about how an accent or dialect can affect an actor's body language or persona. Do you think that this can happen when a person changes a foreign accent to an accent that is more like a native speaker's accent?

Pronunciation ACTIVITIES

Rhythm and Sentence Stress

The rhythm of a language is created by the way that words are stressed in sentences and phrases. To make your English comprehensible, it is even more important to use the stress pattern of English well than it is to pronounce individual sounds correctly. In some languages, the rhythm of stressed and unstressed syllables is very regular. However, in English, the pattern of stressed and unstressed syllables is rather uneven, so when first learning English rhythm, it might seem difficult to predict.

Whereas there are no rules to predict sentence stress 100% of the time, you will be right most of the time if you stress *content words* and reduce *function words*. A content word is a word that carries the most important meaning in a sentence. Nouns, adjectives, verbs, adverbs, question words, and some pronouns (such as "this," "that," "these," "those," "yours," "mine," "ours," "theirs," "myself," yourself," "himself," "herself," "ourselves," and "themselves") are content words and are stressed most of the time.

Example: A DIalect COACH can TRAIN ACTors to SPEAK with an ACcent for a MOVie.

Function words are important grammatically. A function word is a word that is usually reduced and said very quickly. Common function words include articles, prepositions, auxiliary verbs, and pronouns (such as "him," "her," "them," "it," "us," "I," "you," "he," "she," "we," "they," "my," "your," "his," "its," "our," and "their"). Because function words are reduced, many of them are contracted in the following ways.

Contractions with "is":	Contractions with "are":
she's, he's, it's	*we're, you're, they're*
Contractions with "not":	Contractions with "have":
didn't, isn't, couldn't, weren't	*I've, we've, they've*
Contractions with "will":	*Contractions with "has":
I'll, we'll, they'll	*he's, that's, it's*
*Contractions with "would":	*Contractions with "had":
I'd, that'd, he'd	*I'd, she'd, he'd*

* Cannot be written in formal English.

Listen for Content and Function Words

The following excerpts are from the interview with Jessica Drake. In the first, content words have been deleted. In the second, function words have been deleted.

Read the excerpts, and try to guess which words correctly fill in the blanks. Which words are easier to guess?

Excerpt 1: Missing Function Words

I _____ done several. Probably the most well known _____ *Forrest Gump.* That was _____ Alabama dialect. The town itself, Greenbough, _____ completely invented. But _____ I did was, I did interview the writer _____ the novel who _____ some very specific people _____ mind when he wrote _____ And _____ was actually able _____ interview one _____ _____ people the character Forrest _____ based on.

Excerpt 2: Missing Content Words

Oh yeah, _____ . A very good _____ for the body _____ would be Johnny Depp in *Don Juan Demarco.* I _____ absolutely. That _____ is so ingrained with the _____ because you have a _____ there who is actually _____ the accent. He is not _____ . He just _____ he's Spanish and has _____ this whole _____ .

Now listen to the excerpts, and fill in the words that Jessica Drake actually says. You probably discovered that it is easier to guess the function words, but easier to hear the content words.

TALKING POINT

Stress helps you to hear content words when you are taking notes. Focus on noting content words, since they are more important to the main ideas than are the function words.

Predict Rhythm in Sentences

In the following excerpt from the beginning of the interview with Jessica Drake, underline the words that you expect will be stressed. Check your predictions by listening to the first part of the interview. Read the excerpt to a partner or on tape. Practice stressing the words that you underlined and reducing the words that you didn't underline.

> Yes. Or, for a group of actors or for the entire cast, it might be several different dialects all coming into one film. It might be that everybody has to be from the same place that has a very specific regional dialect. Or it could be just one actor who's doing a dialect for that film.

Practice Rhythm

Because function words are unstressed and reduced to such short sounds, it takes an English speaker about the same amount of time to say each of the following five sentences. Read these sentences aloud and at a normal pace. Try to stress the content words and reduce the function words.

KIDS	PLAY	GAMES.
The KIDS	PLAY	GAMES.
The KIDS	are PLAYing	GAMES.
The KIDS	are PLAYing	the GAMES.
The KIDS	will be PLAYing	in the GAMES.

Communicative Pronunciation Practice

Ethnologue: Languages of the World reports that there are 176 living languages used in the United States.[1] The number is higher when languages used in Canada and Mexico are included. In this activity, you will study information about one of these languages and then share the information that you have learned with others in your class.

Follow these steps.

1. Form pairs or small groups with others in your class.

2. Your teacher will assign a text about a language to your group. To find the text, look on this page or on pages 143–145.

3. Read the information quickly. Underline the content words in the information and, in the margins, make quick notes from which to speak. With someone who read the same text, practice telling each other the information until you can do so fluently while stressing the content words with proper rhythm.

4. When you are comfortable with your delivery, form a new group with people who prepared different information.

5. As you present orally to each other, take notes to complete the following chart.

6. Prepare a summary that compares and contrasts the information in the chart. The summary can be written, recorded on tape, or reported to the class as a whole.

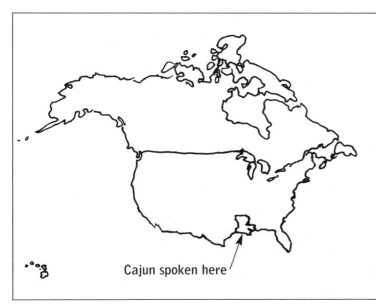

Cajun spoken here

Group A

Name of the language: French Cajun or Acadian[2]
Number of speakers: about 1,000,000
Where spoken: Southern Louisiana
Speakers: The descendants of people who came to Louisiana from French Canada in the eighteenth century. Most speakers born after 1950 are bilingual in English.
Resources in the language: Radio broadcasts, a dictionary, and textbooks on the language are available.

Group	Language	Speakers	Where	Language Facts
A				
B				
C				
D				

TALK It Over!

Definitions

When you listen to someone talk about a subject that is unfamiliar to you, you will probably have to learn specific definitions for new terms that are used in that field. Listening carefully for definitions can help you to understand the speaker better. You can also help your listeners to understand you better by giving clear definitions of any specialized words and terms that you use when you are talking about a specialized topic.

Two kinds of grammatical structures are often used to give definitions.

- **BE Verb Definitions:** The definition begins with the word that is to be defined, followed by "is" or "are" (a form of the verb "be") and then by the definition.

    Example: An accent is the sounds and rhythms with which a person speaks a language.

- **Clause Definitions:** A definition can also be phrased as a noun clause or a relative clause that contains the definition.

    Example: "They have a problem that's called a pin/pen inversion, which means basically when they want to say 'pen' as in 'Hand me a pen to write with,' they will say instead 'Hand me a pin'."

In addition to grammatical structures for giving definitions, you can also use dictionary definitions, word parts, examples, and analogies to define terms.

- **Dictionary:** If you are planning a presentation, you will have time to check a dictionary to help you to define a term for your audience. If you do this, you should always give the name of the dictionary to which you referred.

- **Word Parts:** Many technical words are made of commonly identifiable prefixes, suffixes, and word stems, which you can use to help your audience to understand the term.

- **Use of Examples:** Sometimes the best way to help someone understand an unfamiliar word is to give a good example.

Practice Giving Definitions

Use your notes of the interview with Jessica Drake to write definitions for each of the following terms. Share your definitions with the class, and discuss different ways to define these terms.

1. sound substitution

2. pin/pen inversion

3. upspeak

Present a Definition

Choose a word that is common in your native language but unknown to most speakers of other languages. This could be the name of a special object that is not widely known or an idea for which there is no direct translation in English. Use two or more of the structures and techniques described in the "Talk It Over!" box to explain this word to a small group of your classmates. If you have defined your word well, your classmates should be able to explain the same word to someone else, based on your definition.

Further Practice

Short Narration

On tape or in a small group, tell a funny story that happened to you because of a mistake that you made.

Discussion Questions

In a small group, answer the following discussion questions. Before you begin, refer to the hints for taking part in a discussion on pages 14–16 in Chapter 1.

1. People experience many different feelings when they make pronunciation mistakes. Brainstorm a list of these feelings, and mark the feelings that you have experienced as a result of miscommunication.

2. Imagine that a friend of yours feels embarrassed because people often misunderstand her because of her accent. What advice would you give her?

Chapter 4: Self-Evaluation Chart

Use the following chart to record comments about your progress in mastering each of the following skills that you practiced in this chapter.

	+	−	Teacher's Comments
Note Taking: The Cornell Method • I understand how to use this method. • I am satisfied with my ability to use this method. • I will practice using this method by _____ .			
Speaking Skills: Defining Terms • I understand the techniques used to define terms. • I am satisfied with my ability to define terms. • I will practice these skills by _____ .			
Pronunciation: Rhythm and Stress • I understand the concepts underlying English rhythm. • I am satisfied with my pronunciation of English rhythm. • I will practice rhythm by _____ .			

Biotechnology

5

CHAPTER HIGHLIGHTS

Listening	Note Taking	Pronunciation	Speaking
Main ideas	Outlining	Focal stress	Panel presentations
Details	Summarizing from		
Time order	notes		

Brainstorming

Discuss your answers to the following questions with others in your class, or record your answers on tape.

1. Examine the word "biotechnology," and use your knowledge of English suffixes, roots, and prefixes to decide what you think this word means.

2. Brainstorm a list of terms that you think might be related to the word "biotechnology."

Gathering Information from a Reading

Read the following paragraph, which defines the word "biotechnology." Then discuss the questions that follow.

Biotechnology is a set of powerful tools that employ living organisms (or parts of organisms) to make or modify products, improve plants or animals, or develop microorganisms for specific uses … . Biotechnology has been employed by humans for millennia; traditional applications include the production of beer, cheese, and bread, where yeast and other microorganisms are used to make food. But the recent developments in molecular biology have given biotechnology new meaning, new prominence, and new potential. It is this "new biotechnology" that has captured the attention of scientists, financiers, policy makers, journalists, and the public … . Through the use of advanced tools, such as genetic engineering, biotechnology is expected to have a dramatic effect on the world economy over the next decade.[1]

Discussion Questions

1. According to the article, people have been interested in biotechnology for thousands of years. Why do you think people are so interested in changing living organisms and using them for their own purposes?

2. Based on the definition that you read, what kinds of processes and products do you know about that are examples of "new biotechnology"?

3. The article predicts that in the future, biotechnology will affect our lives in many ways. Make a list of the ways that biotechnology might affect our lives, and determine if these effects are positive or negative.

Listening One
Genetic Research: The Ethical Issues

Before You Listen

Read the following definition of *social impact research*, and then restate it in your own words.

> Social impact research is aimed at understanding the social, cultural, ethical, economic, and legal implications of biotechnology research and its applications.[2]

Indicate whether each of the following possible effects of biotechnology research has social, cultural, ethical, economic, and/or legal implications. Discuss your choices with others in your class. You might find that some of these have several implications.

1. ____ People who cannot have biological children could clone themselves in order to have a child who carries their genes.

2. ____ An insurance company might deny a customer insurance because a test showed that the customer might get a genetic disease.

3. ____ A tomato plant can be genetically engineered to produce more tomatoes and to be resistant to damaging diseases.

4. ____ Parents could genetically select which of their traits and characteristics they would like their children to have.

5. ____ The government could decide to make illegal certain biotechnological processes, such as cloning or research on human genes.

6. ____ A doctor and patient must decide whether to test a patient for a genetic disease that has no cure.

Listen for Main Ideas

Listen to the lecture by Dr. Edward Keyserlingk, and in your own words, describe the two problems that he says could be caused by this new ability to know about an individual's genetic information.

Problem 1:

_____

Problem 2:

_____

Listen for Details

Listen again to the lecture by Edward Keyserlingk to learn the correct answer that will complete each of the following sentences. Make notes of the answers, and then use your notes to write grammatically correct endings for the sentences. Compare your answers with a partner's. There may be several correct ways to complete each sentence.

1. The genetic tests discussed in this lecture are used to show

   _____

2. It is uncertain whether people should be told that they have a genetic marker for some diseases because

   _____

3. If employers or insurance companies had access to information from genetic marker tests

   _____

4. Because it is becoming increasingly difficult to keep medical information secure, some people wonder

   _____

5. Genetic information has potential benefits for people, but

   _____

After You Listen

Discuss the following questions with a group of your classmates.

1. What are some of the benefits of genetic-susceptibility tests for certain diseases? What are some disadvantages?

2. Create three guidelines about the disclosure of the results of these tests that you would want doctors and researchers to follow.

3. If your doctor suggested one of these tests for a disease that cannot yet be cured, would you want to take the test and know the results? Why or why not?

Listening Two
Biosafety: An Introductory Lecture

Before You Listen

With a group of your classmates, list in the following chart possible dangers related to the types of biotechnology shown in the pictures. Consider issues such as safety, health, and ethical concerns. Then make a list of ways by which these dangers can be avoided.

Type of Biotechnology	Possible Dangers	Ways to Avoid This Danger
Create a tomato that will stay fresh a long time		
Give cows growth hormone so that they will produce more milk		
Clone a sheep or other mammal		
Create a virus for scientific study		

Terminology

If you want to understand an academic lecture better, you must understand some of the basic terminology that the lecturer will use. You can prepare by reading the definitions of special terms before an academic class. For the lecture in this activity, you will need to understand the following basic biological terms.

biosafety*   **cancer**   **genetics**

recombinant DNA*   **DNA and RNA**

*These terms are defined by the lecturer at the beginning of the lecture.

1. Note what you think the meanings of the terms are.

2. If you are not sure of a meaning, use your knowledge of word parts to guess, if possible.

3. If, after you follow these steps, you are still unsure about the meaning of a term, check a dictionary.

4. Compare your answers with a classmate's.

Listen for Time Order

Listen to the lecture about biosafety by Dr. Peter Keating. He often uses dates to help you to understand how the modern idea of biosafety developed from the 1960s on. Listen to the lecture, and above each of the dates on the following time line make note of what happened during this period in the history of biosafety.

| 1960s | End of the 1960s | Mid-1970s | Since 1976 | Mid-1980s |

Listen for Details

Listen to the lecture again to hear the answers to the following questions.

1. What kinds of experiments caused biosafety to become an important issue?

_____

2. What is the name of the cancer-causing virus used in some of these experiments?

_____

3. In the United States, what organization determines whether an experiment is dangerous?

_____

4. From the point of view of biosafety, what kinds of experiments are the most dangerous?

_____

5. What is the strictest kind of laboratory used for the most dangerous experiments?

_____

6. Why is this sort of facility safe?

_____

7. How many accidents have there been that involve disease-causing organisms created in biological experiments?

_____

8. What disease did TASS accuse U.S. scientists of creating?

_____

NOTE
Taking

Outlining

When speakers plan a formal presentation such as a lecture, they will often organize the presentation in outline form so that the information follows a logical pattern that listeners can understand more easily.

An outline uses numbers, letters, and spacing to illustrate the logical structure of main ideas, supporting points, and details. An outline is usually organized by using a special system of numbering that shows main points and subpoints.

When you are taking notes as you listen to a speaker, try to follow the outline format as closely as you can. In that way, you can fill in missing information and details immediately after the lecture by asking the speaker or by checking with other listeners.

 The following is an example of notes that a native speaker of English took while listening to the first part of the talk by Dr. Keyserlingk. Listen to the interview again, and follow along to see how these note-taking principles were followed.

Biomedical ethics
I.   Data being generated
A. Susceptibilities, not genetic problems
B. Example: Marker for Alzheimer's
1. Don't know when someone will get it
2. Don't know how serious
3. No cure
II.   Ethical problems
A. Do you tell people? Information may interest
1. Employers -- deny employment
2. Insurance companies -- deny insurance

An outline of the lecture on biosafety follows. Only some of the major points of the outline are included. As you listen to the lecture, try to use outline format to take notes on the information in the lecture.

An Introduction to Biosafety

I. Introduction

    A.   Definition

II. Is an experiment dangerous? Rules and Guidelines for DNA research

III. Laboratory precautions for "dangerous" experiments

IV. Do the rules work?

V. Next class: Possible dangers of current experiments

After You Listen

Summarizing from Notes

Taking notes can help you to remember the information that you hear, but you will remember even more if you review and summarize your notes a few hours after you take them. Use your notes, and follow these steps to complete the lecture summary that follows.

1. Review the notes that you made.

2. Cover the notes. Do not look at them while you write so that you are forced to use different words and structures to express the ideas.

3. Write a topic sentence that introduces the main idea of the lecture.

4. For each main point in the lecture, write a sentence that restates this idea. Leave out details, and focus on the main ideas only.

5. Rewrite the summary as many times as you must to make each sentence clear, concise, and original.

When it became possible to combine genetic information from different organisms, people worried that a disease-causing organism might escape from a laboratory, so biosafety became an important issue.

_____

_____

_____

_____

_____

_____

_____

_____

TALKING POINT

Summarizing can also help you to increase your vocabulary and improve your grammar because when you summarize, you must use your own words, phrases, and grammatical structures.

Pronunciation ACTIVITIES

Focal Stress

In Chapter 4, you learned that, as a general rule, English rhythm is produced by stressing content words and reducing function words. Another important feature of English rhythm is *focal stress*. Focal stress is extra stress given to one word in each thought group; it is used to emphasize important concepts and ideas or to signal a shift in topic. Focal stress can even change the meaning of a sentence. For example, in each of the following sentences, placing focal stress on the words in CAPITAL LETTERS changes the meaning of the sentence.

1. I BOUGHT a NEW TEXTBOOK. (I purchased a book for a class.)

2. I BOUGHT a NEW TEXTBOOK. (Because I lost my first textbook, I bought a new one.)

3. I BOUGHT A NEW TEXTBOOK. (I bought only one book, not several.)

4. I BOUGHT a NEW TEXTBOOK. (My friend didn't loan me hers, so I bought a book.)

5. I BOUGHT a NEW TEXTBOOK. (You still didn't buy a book for class, but I did.)

Of course, the context of the conversation determines focal stress. In the following dialog, words are stressed to show shifts in the topics of conversation. Again, CAPITAL LETTERS mark focal stress. Syllables receiving regular sentence stress are marked with SMALL CAPITAL LETTERS. Syllables in lowercase letters are reduced.

A: I'm HAVING TROUBLE with the HOMEwork. Did you DO it yet?

B: I DID SOME of it. WHICH homework?

A: The biOlogy HOMEWORK. It's REALLY HARD.

B: Did you READ the HANDout?

A: WHICH handout?

B: The HANDOUT with the DIagRAM. The PROFESSOR GAVE it to us in CLASS.

A: I wasn't IN CLASS TODAY.

B: THAT's WHY you THINK the HOMEWORK's HARD!

It is also very common for lecturers to stress words to help draw the audience's attention to special terms that are important to understand and to shifts in topic.

Listen for Focal Stress

Listen to the following excerpt from Peter Keating's lecture on biosafety, paying attention to the words that receive focal stress. Discuss the questions that follow with others in your class.

> The NATional INstitutes of HEALTH has diVIDed LABoratories into FOUR KINDs. The LOWest KIND is your REGular BASic biOlogy LAB, like the ONES you WORK in in introDUCtory COURSes in biOlogy. At the OTHer END, the STRICTest TYPE of LABoratory is WHAT is CALLed a P4 LABoratory. THIS TYPE of LABoratory did not EXIST before exPERiments that maNIpulated and recomBINed DNA and RNA beGAN. The P4 LABoratory was inVENTed for THESE TYPES of exPERiments.

Discussion Questions

1. Look at the words that receive focal stress. Why does Peter Keating emphasize these words?

2. How can paying attention to focal stress make you a more efficient listener? How can using focal stress make you a more effective speaker? How can you use your awareness of focal stress to make your notes more complete and accurate?

Listen to the excerpt again, and read along with Peter Keating, stressing the same words that he does.

Practice Hearing Focal Stress

In the following excerpt, words are stressed to help the listener focus on the main topics of the listening. Listen to the excerpt from the lecture, and underline the words that receive focal stress.

> Biosafety wasn't a major issue until the 1960s. It was then that experiments first began using recombinant DNA. (Recombinant DNA is genetic material taken from one individual or species and inserted into or combined with that of another species.) In the sixties, work was being carried out using what was called the SV 40 virus. The SV 40 virus is a virus that causes cancer. The virus can be introduced into any kind of cell, including a human cell, and cause malignancy—that is, make a healthy cell cancerous.

Listen to the excerpt again, and read along with Peter Keating, stressing the same words that he does.

Practice Pronouncing Focal Stress

One partner will look at the picture on this page, and the other partner will look at the picture on page 146. Although the pictures are similar, there are at least ten differences between them. Without looking at each other's pictures, describe your pictures and try to locate and list these ten differences. Use focal stress to emphasize the differences that you find.

Example: A: My picture has two people at a TAble.
                        B: Mine TOO. My table is ROUND.
                        A: I have a SQUARE table.

Communicative Pronunciation Practice

Many things made possible by biotechnology were not even imaginable twenty years ago. What do you think technology will make possible in the future?

     Complete each of the following sentences with a prediction. Then underline the word that receives focal stress in each sentence.

Example: Next year, a cure for the common <u>cold</u> will be discovered.

1. Next year: _____ .

2. In twenty years: _____ .

3. In 100 years: _____ .

With a group of your classmates, take turns reading your predictions. After one person reads a prediction, the next person must agree or disagree with the prediction and add a similar prediction. Be sure to pronounce focal stress correctly.

Example: A: Next year, we will have a cure for the common COLD.
               B: I don't think that we will cure the common COLD next
                    year, but I think that we WILL find a cure for cancer.

            Or
            A: Next year, we will have a cure for the common COLD.
            B: I don't think that we will cure the common cold NEXT
                year, but I think that we will find a cure for the cold in
                TWENTY years.

            Or
            A: Next year, we will have a cure for the common COLD.
            B: I agree, and I think that we'll discover a cure for
                CANCER, too.

TALK
It Over!

Panel Presentations

Often in the academic and business worlds, several people must work as a team to present information on a topic. When people work as a team, it is important that each person know what topic he or she is responsible for presenting. One of the best ways to organize group presentations is to make an outline of all of the information to be presented and then assign each speaker to present a part of an outline.

Steps for Planning a Presentation

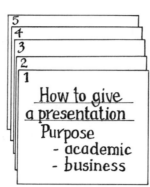

1. Write down the main ideas of your part of the presentation. Put each step at the top of a note card or piece of paper.

2. Make notes on the note card or paper about what you want to say about each step.

3. Be sure to plan to define any special terms that might be unfamiliar to your audience. (Check the "Talk It Over!" box in Chapter 4 if you need help planning a definition.)

4. Plan the introduction and conclusion for the presentation. You might want to assign one group member to give this part of the presentation, but all group members should agree on what is to be said.

5. Put all of the notes in order. Write a large number 1 at the top of the first note card, 2 at the top of the second card, and so on. This will help you to quickly make sure that your notes are in order before you make your presentation.

6. Practice your part of the presentation, and time yourself to see if you are within your time limit. You might find it helpful to record yourself giving the presentation and then listen to see what improvements you can make. Practice using correct rhythm and sentence stress.

After presenting your panel presentation to your classmates, evaluate your presentations using the evaluation form on page 151.

As a group, follow these steps to plan and present a group presentation to others in your class.

1. Choose a topic about which everyone in your group can speak. To help you to think of ideas, look in the library for articles on biotechnology, in magazines such as *Science, National Geographic, Time,* and *Newsweek,* or do an Internet search for keywords such as cloning, bio-engineered foods, the human genome project, medical ethics, or a biotechnology topic of interest to you.

2. Gather information from the library or the Internet.

3. Create a general outline of the presentation.

4. Assign each group member a portion of the outline to present. Each speaker should organize his or her part of the presentation.

5. Practice your part of the presentation on your own and with your group.

6. Present your presentation to others in the class. For extra note-taking practice, take notes as you listen to classmates' presentations.

TALKING POINT

On your note cards, mark special terms that you want to emphasize and shifts from one topic to the next. Use focal stress on these words to help your audience focus on the important parts of your presentation.

Further Practice

Listen to a Lecture

Colleges and communities often sponsor lectures by guest speakers on topics of interest to the community. Usually these lectures are free and open to the public and are advertised in a special section of a local newspaper or on college and community bulletin boards.

Find out what lectures are coming up in your community, or find a professor who will allow you to attend a lecture on a topic of interest to you. Fill in the following chart, and take notes on the lecture. After the lecture, summarize the most interesting and important ideas from the lecture for a group of your classmates.

Lecturer's name: _____

Title of the lecture: _____

Date, time, and location of the lecture: _____

Which of the following lecture techniques did the lecturer use to organize the information in the lecture?

_____   Outline structure

_____   Focal stress to signal topic changes

_____   Visual aids

_____   Focal stress to emphasize important terms

_____   Gestures

Chapter 5: Self-Evaluation Chart

Use the following chart to record comments about your progress in mastering each of the following skills that you practiced in this chapter.

	+	–	Teacher's Comments
Note Taking: Outlining and Summarizing • I understand how to outline and summarize. • I am satisfied with my ability to use these skills. • I will practice outlining and summarizing by _____ .			
Speaking Skills: Group Presentations • I am satisfied with my participation in this presentation. • I need to keep working on these presentation skills: _____ .			
Pronunciation: Focal Stress • I understand the concept of focal stress. • I am satisfied with my ability to hear and pronounce focal stress. • I will practice focal stress in my everyday speech by _____ .			

Roots: Living in Two Cultures

CHAPTER HIGHLIGHTS

Listening	Note Taking	Pronunciation	Speaking
Main ideas Details Predictions	Idea mapping	Intonation to signal complete and incomplete thoughts	Presenting to a small group

Brainstorming

Discuss your answers to the following questions with others in your class, or record your answers on tape.

1. When you move to a new culture, is it important to assimilate into that culture or to become like the people in that culture?

2. Is it important for you to preserve your original culture?

3. Can you do both?

Gathering Information from Tables

The data in the following table, from the U.S. Immigration and Naturalization Service, shows what countries people come from to visit the United States for each of four different purposes.[1] Study the data in the table, and then discuss the questions that follow.

Top Ten Countries of Origin of People Who Came to the United States for Four Different Purposes

To Immigrate	As a Tourist	As a Temporary Worker	As a Student
Mexico	Japan	United Kingdom	Japan
Philippines	United Kingdom	Canada	Korea
India	Germany	Japan	China*
Vietnam	Mexico	Germany	India
China*	France	India	Germany
Dominican Republic	Brazil	Mexico	Thailand
Cuba	Korea	France	Brazil
Ukraine	Italy	China*	Mexico
Russia	China*	Russia	Indonesia
Jamaica	Netherlands	Brazil	United Kingdom

*Includes Taiwan.

Discussion Questions

1. How long do you think that people in each of these four categories plan to stay in the United States?

2. Pick one country from each of the four categories. Based on what you know about the historical, political, social, and economic situations in these countries, why do you think that people from each of these countries are coming to the United States for the specified purpose?

3. In your opinion, how important or desirable is assimilation into a new culture for people who come to that culture for

   a.   immigration?

   b.   tourism?

   c   temporary work?

   d.   study?

Listening One
Values Under Siege

Before You Listen

What cultural differences do people encounter when they move to a new culture to study, to work, or to live permanently? Which of the following would you be willing to change or adapt? Why or why not? Discuss your answers with others in your class.

	Willing to Change	Why or Why Not
Daily Routines		
Traditions		
Values		
Religion		
Other:		

Listen for Main Ideas

In this listening, Nancy Odeh, a young Palestinian woman who is studying at a university in North America, talks about some cultural difficulties that she has encountered while living abroad and how her time abroad has affected her relationship to her culture and religion.

 Preview the following statements, and then listen to hear whether the statements below are true or false. Circle the correct answer.

1. It is getting easier for her to live abroad.

                                                                    True   False

2. She thinks that performing her religious duties while she is abroad is different and more difficult than when she is at home with family.

                                                                    True   False

3. Contact with friends and family helps her through difficult times.

                                                                    True   False

4. Living abroad has changed her attitude toward her culture in many ways.   True   False

Listen for Details

 Listen again, and complete the following chart. Write the information in note form.

	Nancy Odeh
Difficulties that she encountered when adjusting to life abroad	
Things that have helped her to adjust to those difficulties	
Other people's reaction to her cultural differences	
The effect on her attitude toward her original culture	

After You Listen

Think about the issues discussed in the previous section, and fill in the following chart for yourself. The new "culture" that you think about could be a new country, a new school, a new neighborhood, or another culture. Then use your answers in the chart as a guide while you discuss these issues with a group of classmates. Be prepared to summarize your group's answers for the class as a whole.

	You
Difficulties that you encountered when adjusting to a new culture	
Things that have helped you to adjust to those difficulties	
Other people's reaction to your cultural differences	
The effect on your attitude toward your original culture	

Listening Two
New Land/Old Roots

This is a conversation among three American immigrants. Po Yi came with her family from Korea to New York. She's in law school. Dorota is from Poland, has been in the United States for five years, and studies fashion design. Carmen is from Venezuela. She works for the airlines, and her parents live in Florida.

Predicting Before You Listen

Read each of the following ideas, and mark an X in column one if you think that any of the three women might talk about the idea in the recording.

TALKING POINT

> Thinking about what you expect to hear before you actually listen to someone can help you to be a better listener. This strategy is called "predicting."

Predicted	Actually Discussed	
_____	_____	You can have a different culture when you live with family members than when you live alone.
_____	_____	It is not difficult to adapt to a new culture.
_____	_____	My relationship with my parents is an important part of my culture.
_____	_____	It's important to preserve my original culture and to teach it to my children.
_____	_____	When I'm not immersed in my culture, I might lose a little bit of it, but I can never forget my roots.
_____	_____	I have to go home every year, or I will forget my original culture.
_____	_____	When adults move to a new country, assimilating will make their lives easier, but the process of assimilation is difficult.

Listen to Check Predictions

Listen to the recording, and in column two mark an X next to the ideas that the women actually do discuss.

NOTE
Taking

Idea Mapping

In this style of note taking, you make a visual representation of the information that you hear and show how the information is interrelated. Idea mapping is useful when speakers are discussing many aspects of one concept and when the relationships between ideas are of special importance.

   To make an idea map, listen carefully for main ideas. Write these in empty spaces on your notepaper. Near the main ideas, write the details related to each main idea. Use circles, squares, lines, arrows, and other symbols to show the relationships between the different ideas.

   The following is an example of notes that a native speaker of English took while listening to the talk by Nancy Odeh. If you had made an idea map of this talk, your idea map might look different. The important thing about this style of note taking is that you adapt it to help you to remember the information that you heard.

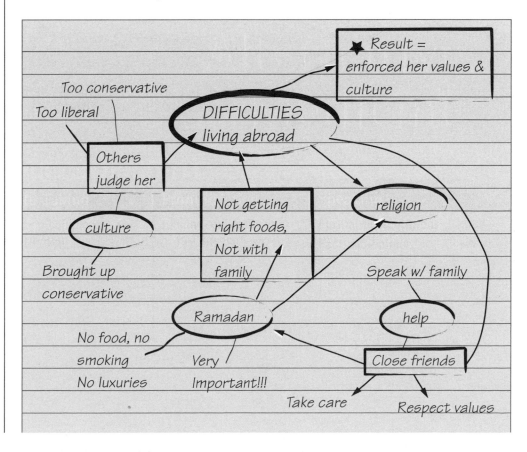

Listen to the conversation between Dorota, Po, and Carmen again. As you listen, create an idea map which shows the main ideas and related details that the women discuss. Use the following map to get started, or use your own paper to create your map.

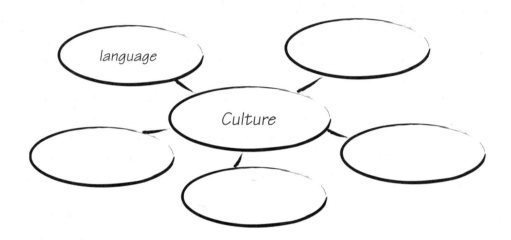

After You Listen

Using Analogies to Get Your Point Across

An *analogy* is an explanation of a difficult concept that is made easier by comparing it to something from the real world. Dorota uses an analogy when she says "If you come here in your twenties, just like I did, I was twenty-two, you are like fully grown tree which was just transplanted to alien soil. And you have to climb all the economical and social and cultural ladders all over again."

What does Dorota mean? Think about how you felt when you were in a new situation such as entering a new culture or starting a new school. Some common analogies for this situation are "I feel like a fish out of water" and "I feel like a motherless child."

An analogy can express ideas in a way that conveys emotions or gives a colorful impression. Carmen uses an analogy to describe how she is different from some other Americans. She says, "I don't know what it's like to be apple pie and baseball. That's just not me. For me, it's *salsa y merengue.*"

Think of an analogy that explains how you felt when you were in a new place, such as when you moved or started a new school. Write your analogy on the following lines.

When I _____

I felt like _____ .

Make a comparison like this about your culture: What two things from your culture are like apple pie and baseball are to many Americans? Write your comparison on the following line.

For me, it's _____ .

After you have prepared your analogies, share them with others in your class.

TALKING POINT

Use analogies to express your ideas in a more interesting way. Analogies can also help you to express an idea when you don't know the precise words needed to explain the idea directly.

Pronunciation ACTIVITIES

Using Intonation to Signal Complete and Incomplete Thoughts

Intonation is not used only for questions and statements. English speakers also use intonation to signal when they are finished speaking and when they plan to continue. Slight rises and drops in pitch near the end of a thought group indicate that more information will follow. A sharp drop in pitch at the end of a thought group means that the speaker has completed a thought.* A second speaker might hear this signal and take the opportunity to speak, or the original speaker might continue with a new idea.

In the following example, the line marks the intonation that Po uses when she speaks. Notice that the intonation for each thought group rises or falls only slightly until Po has completed her idea. The last thought group has a steep fall in pitch.

Example: Yes, in the sense that I always have this separate culture

at home, so when I'm at home I have to be Korean.

It is important to learn to hear and use intonation correctly for the following reasons.

1. Unless you have been asked a question, it is rude to begin speaking while someone is using rising intonation. You will probably interrupt the speaker.

2. You can more actively participate in discussions, since you'll be able to hear when it is appropriate to speak.

3. Others will feel more comfortable talking to you if you use intonation correctly. They will feel that it is "less work" to talk to you, and you will have more opportunities to speak English with others.

Showing whether one is finished speaking is especially important when saying several items in a list. A deeper drop in pitch occurs when a person says the last item in a list.

Example: The students in my class speak Spanish, Swahili,

Japanese, and Malaysian.

* As demonstrated in Chapter 2, a sharp increase in pitch indicates a completed yes/no question.

If the list is incomplete, or if the items in the list are just examples of many more items in this group, the intonation rises slightly on every item in the list.

Example: The students in my class speak fifteen different languages,

such as Spanish, Swahili, Japanese, Malaysian …

Practice Using Intonation

Listen to each of the following sentences. After you hear each sentence, circle "Continue" if you think that the speaker will continue this thought and circle "Completed" if you think that the speaker has completed the thought.

1. Yes, in the sense that I always have this separate culture at home

    Continue   Completed

2. But I don't feel that it's unnatural

    Continue   Completed

3. When I'm with my friends, it doesn't mean that I become a different person

    Continue   Completed

4. I try, for example, to celebrate holidays

    Continue   Completed

5. Also, during Easter time, I do paint eggs

    Continue   Completed

6. Part of my life was just more mainstream

    Continue   Completed

7. I have a U.S. passport, I love this country, it's a wonderful place, but I'm still from Venezuela, and I still have family in Venezuela, and I go back every year

    Continue   Completed

8. I think that when you're a foreigner, you'll always be a foreigner

    Continue   Completed

9. I mean, that's just not me

    Continue   Completed

10. If you come here in your twenties, just like I did; I was twenty-two

    Continue   Completed

Practice Using Intonation

 Listen to these sentences again, and repeat them along with the speaker. Try to match the speaker's pauses and intonation as you speak. Repeat this exercise until you feel that you are pronouncing the sentences with the same intonation patterns as the speaker.

1. Yes, in the sense that I always have this separate culture at home

2. But I don't feel that it's unnatural

3. When I'm with my friends, it doesn't mean that I become a different person

4. I try, for example, to celebrate holidays

5. Also, during Easter time, I do paint eggs

6. Part of my life was just more mainstream

7. I have a U.S. passport, I love this country, it's a wonderful place, but I'm still from Venezuela, and I still have family in Venezuela, and I go back every year

8. I think that when you're a foreigner, you'll always be a foreigner

9. I mean, that's just not me

10. If you come here in your twenties, just like I did; I was twenty-two

For additional practice, listen to these sentences again. Draw lines to show the pitch rises and falls that you hear. Listen as often as you need to in order to feel that you have marked the intonation correctly.

Practice Using Intonation to Indicate Complete and Incomplete Lists

With a partner or in a small group, use rising and falling arrows to mark the intonation patterns that match the meaning of each of the following sentences. Then, read the dialogs with the correct intonation patterns. Make sure that each group member gets a chance to practice reading the second part. Be prepared to explain why you chose the intonation pattern that you did.

a. Mel: What did you do this weekend?
    Bobby: Oh, I washed my car and went to the library and slept. That's it.

    Mel: What did you do this weekend?
    Bobby: Oh, I washed my car and went to the library, slept …
              different things, but nothing special.

b. Lynn: What do we need from the grocery store?
    Jerry: We need lots of things: flour, bread, milk, eggs, sugar …
              all the basic things.

    Lynn: What do we need from the grocery store?
    Jerry: There are five things on the list: flour, bread, milk, eggs,
              and sugar.

c. Pat: What countries have you visited?
    Stacy: Just three. India, Malaysia, and Germany.

    Pat: What countries have you visited?
    Stacy: India, Malaysia, Germany … I've been to so many, it's hard
              to remember them all.

d. Sam: What would you like for breakfast?
    Marian: I think I want either cereal and milk or bacon and eggs.

    Sam: What would you like for breakfast?
    Marian: Oh, cereal and milk or bacon and eggs … Anything is OK.

Communicative Pronunciation Practice

Test your ability to hear and use the falling intonation that signals a completed statement by playing the game "Interruption." Here are the rules for the game.

1. Plan to discuss the following question with a group of four or five classmates:

   What are the best ways to adapt or adjust when starting a new job, entering a new school, or moving to a new town?

2. Individually, plan an answer to this question. Feel free to give ideas and express opinions, but be sure that your answer has several thought groups.

3. Take turns giving your responses. As each group member gives a response, other group members listen to the speaker's intonation.

   a. When a sharp drop in the speaker's intonation indicates that the speaker is finished, raise your hand.

   b. Be careful not to "interrupt" the speaker by raising your hand before you hear the correct falling intonation.

   c. The first person to raise his or her hand at the correct time gets to choose the person who will be the next speaker.

TALK It Over!

Presenting to a Small Group

In academic and business situations, there are many occasions when it is important to be able to present information to a small group of people. These presentations might be less formal than an individual presentation in front of a large audience, in the sense that you might be sitting while you present and you might not be required to have elaborate visual aids. Nonetheless, careful planning and organization of ideas is necessary in order to communicate successfully in small group presentations. The techniques that you learn for such presentations can also help you to prepare for more-formal presentations to larger audiences.

Choosing a Specific Topic

You will need to choose a very specific topic so that the information can be presented clearly in the time allowed.

In the following list, put an X next to topics that you believe are specific enough to be explained in about five minutes. Put an O next to topics that you think are too broad to be explained in five minutes.

_____ How to change the oil in your car

_____ The history of the modern Olympics

_____ How to study for the TOEFL

_____ How to check a book out of the library

_____ How to make pancakes

_____ How to do a chemistry experiment

Compare your answers with others in your group. For the topics that you felt were too broad, try to think of a related subtopic that could be presented in five minutes.

Choose a Topic for Your Presentation

List on the following lines three topics that you could present to a small group. Be careful to choose topics that are specific enough to be explained in about five minutes.

_____

_____

_____

Discuss the topics with a classmate to help you to select one for your presentation. Write the topic on a piece of paper, and present it to your teacher for approval. Plan your presentation following the steps in the "Talk it Over!" box in Chapter 5. Present your presentation to a small group of your classmates.

Responsibilities of the Speaker

- Use your notes to help you to speak fluently, but do not read your notes.
- Speak at a normal pace and loud enough so that the audience can hear you easily.
- Make eye contact with each person in your small group during the course of your talk.
- Use gestures and body language to emphasize important points.
- Animate your presentation by asking the audience questions and inviting them to ask you questions.

Responsibilities of the Audience

- Take notes on your classmates' presentations by using the Cornell method of note taking.
- As you take notes, write down any questions that come to mind. Ask these questions at the end of the presentation.
- Participate actively when the speaker asks questions and in the discussion after each presentation.

Further Practice

Group Discussion

In a part of the interview that you did not hear, Po and Carmen talk about how their culture affects their relationships with their parents. Read the following comments from the interview, and then discuss the questions that follow.

Anthea: When you think about aspects of Korean culture that may have followed you to the United States, are there many that come to mind?

Po: I think a sense of family that's strong, that familial bond that is still there. It would be presumptuous to say that there is no sense of family in American society. But in Korea, it's even stronger. You know that close-knit family unit that you have.

Anthea: Carmen, what do you think reminds you most that you're Latin?

Carmen: My parents are very, very important to me. No matter what they do … I still love them. I think that might play a little bit into the Latin culture versus what I've seen in America or in other parts of the world, where children don't have relationships with their parents … I don't think I've met or know of a Latin individual that doesn't have some sort of relationship with the family, whereas here, in this country, I've met a lot of people, not only from this country, but from Europe as well … who don't have a relationship with parents.

Anthea: Do you think that comes from the experience of leaving a place and needing something to keep you together?

Po: I don't think so. I think when Koreans come to the States, they tend to … the family unit tends to disperse. Whereas in Korea, they're still together. There's the three-generation household. Here it's not so much that. People move out, families try to stay together, but it ends up being not that way, especially as the American culture gets merged with Korean culture. The younger generation wants to move out, doesn't want to stay with the family core.

Discussion Questions

1. What are parent/child relationships like in your native culture? How do they differ from the family relationships in other cultures with which you are familiar?

2. What aspects of your culture have followed you or your family to the United States or Canada? What parts of American or Canadian culture have merged with your original culture?

3. What assumptions do the speakers make about American or Canadian culture? Do you agree or disagree?

Listening in the Real World

Television does not give a perfect picture of a country's culture, but it can give you some cultural clues. In this activity, you will watch parts of television shows to find clues about the culture in which you live.

Watch a television show to gather information about North American culture. Several members of the class may watch a show together, or the class may videotape a show and watch it later together in class. As you watch, make notes on the answers to the following questions.

About Relationships

1. If there are children in this show, how do they talk to their parents? How do the adults talk to each other? Do they speak respectfully? Angrily?

2. What topics do men and women discuss with one another? Did any of the topics they talk about surprise you?

3. How would you describe the people who are friends with the main characters in the show? What kind of relationships do friends seem to have?

About Food and Clothing

1. What kinds of food do people eat? How often do you see people eating in this show? When do they eat, and where do you see them eating?

2. What kinds of clothes do people in this show wear? Are they stylish? Do the people dress appropriately for people their age? Do they wear any strange or unusual clothing?

About the Situations That the Characters Experience

1. What funny situations are the characters in? What makes the characters in the show laugh? What makes the audience laugh?

2. What sad or scary situations are the characters in? What problems do they have? Are the problems solved? How? Do you think that the solutions are realistic?

Describe and discuss the cultural clues that you found in the shows that you watched together, or record a summary on tape.

Chapter 6: Self-Evaluation Chart

Use the following chart to record comments about your progress in mastering each of the following skills that you practiced in this chapter.

	+	–	Teacher's Comments
Note Taking: Idea Mapping • I understand this skill. • I am satisfied with my ability to use this skill. • I plan to use this skill again.			
Speaking Skills: Presenting to a Small Group • I am satisfied with my ability to present to a small group. • I plan to practice this skill by _____ .			
Pronunciation Intonation: Complete and Incomplete Thoughts • I understand how intonation signals when a thought is complete. • I am satisfied with my ability to use this concept. • I try to practice this in my everyday speaking.			

Making
It Work

7

Brainstorming

Discuss your answer to the following question with others in your class, or record your answer on tape.

If you were planning to start your own business or launch your career, what steps would you take to help be sure that you would be successful?

Self-Evaluation

The U.S. Department of Commerce has developed the following question-naire[1] so that people can determine whether they have the characteristics shared by most successful entrepreneurs.

Do You Have What It Takes?

Answer the following questions as honestly as possible. Remember, honesty is on the list of characteristics.

Yes	No		
____	____	1.	Do you have the capacity for hard work and long hours?
____	____	2.	Are you a self-starter?
____	____	3.	Are you a leader and team-builder?
____	____	4.	Are you a good planner?
____	____	5.	Are you honest and trustworthy?
____	____	6.	Do you stick with things?
____	____	7.	Are you confident without being egotistical?
____	____	8.	Are you flexible and adapt to change easily?
____	____	9.	Do you have a strong desire to succeed?
____	____	10.	Are you comfortable taking risks?

You should have answered "yes" to each of the questions. If you did answer "no" to any of the questions, then you should examine why you answered "no" and find ways to improve on those areas.

Now discuss the characteristics of entrepreneurs with a group of class-mates. Do you agree that these are the characteristics of successful busi-ness people? Why or why not? What other characteristics do you believe help a person to be a successful entrepreneur?

Listening One
The Price of Success

Diana Soviero is an internationally acclaimed opera singer who is famous for her roles in operas such as "La Traviata," "Madame Butterfly," and "Pagliacci." To be as successful as she is, Soviero spent many years studying, performing, and traveling.

Before You Listen

In this interview, Diana Soviero uses several idiomatic phrases to describe her job and her character. Before you listen, try to match the idiom with its meaning.

1. ____ that keeps me on my toes
2. ____ you just keep plugging away
3. ____ it's called stick-to-itiveness
4. ____ guts
5. ____ shop-a-holic
6. ____ Is success what it's cracked up to be?

a. Is it as good as people say it is?

b. It keeps me very busy and active.

c. a person who is addicted to shopping

d. you keep working at it

e. courage and strong inner emotions

f. the ability to keep trying until you get what you want

Listen for Main Ideas

Listen to the interview with Diana Soviero to hear the answers to these questions. Then compare your answers with a partner's.

1. List three things that Soviero believes have helped to make her successful.

   _____

2. What advice does Soviero give to young people who have a dream?

   _____

Listen for Details

Listen again to the interview with Diana Soviero, and answer the following questions.

1. Why does Diana Soviero need a great deal of physical endurance?

   _____

2. Why does she think that she became successful in her career?

   _____

3. List the sacrifices that she made and the things that she has deprived herself of in order to be successful.

   _____

4. Does she think that her success was worth all of the things that it cost her?

   _____

5. According to Diana Soviero, what do opera singers and athletes have in common?

   _____

After You Listen

Discuss the following questions with a group of classmates.

1. Look again at the questionnaire at the beginning of this chapter. Based on what you heard in this interview, which of the characteristics listed in the questionnaire do you think Diana Soviero has?

2. Diana Soviero's advice to young people with a dream is to "Follow it. Do anything you can to make that dream come true. And if you want it and wish for it, you'll get it." Do you agree with her? Why or why not?

Listening Two
The Business of Rock-n-Roll

David King is a respected rock guitar player in Los Angeles, but he had a dream of starting his own business, a record label. He has, and has released a number of titles in a partnership with the recording giant, Atlantic. Listen to this chat that *Talk It Over!* had with David King, and find out how a rock musician is making it in the world of business.

Before You Listen

David King uses several idiomatic phrases and a lot of figurative language during this interview. To help you to understand the interview, try to match the phrase from the interview in the left-hand column with the phrase that has the same meaning in the right-hand column. Compare your answers with your classmates'.

Group One

1. _____ I saw a lot of opportunities fall through the cracks.

2. _____ You point your finger at everybody.

3. _____ This is a great window of opportunity.

4. _____ You've got a good head on your shoulders.

a. This is a chance, a possibility.

b. You are intelligent; you think clearly.

c. Chances to make money passed by, and no one took action.

d. You blame everyone.

Group Two

5. _____ Keep your eyes open.

6. _____ My gut instinct is usually pretty good.

7. _____ I've heard of the great deals he has struck.

8. _____ The nuts and bolts of the deal

e. I get good results when I follow my feelings about something.

f. Pay attention.

g. The details of an agreement

h. I've heard about the good business contracts he has negotiated.

Group Three

9. ____ We all sink or swim together.   i. It is very competitive.

10. ____ Anything above and beyond that would just be gravy.   j. They care about us, but they want us to solve our own problems.

11. ____ It is so cutthroat.

12. ____ It's more of like a tough love approach.   k. Anything else we get is nice, but it is not necessary.

     l. We succeed or fail together.

Listen for Main Ideas

 Listen to the interview to hear the answers to the following questions.

1. Why did David King decide to start his own record label?

   _____

2. What was his job before he started the record label?

   _____

3. How did he prepare for his meeting with the president of Atlantic Records?

   _____

4. Why does a big company such as Atlantic Records want to support a small record label?

   _____

5. What kinds of difficulties has David King encountered in running his own record label?

   _____

NOTE
Taking

Paragraph-Style Notes

Some students prefer to take notes in paragraph style. In this note-taking style, you write down and underline a main idea. Then under it, you add details about the idea as quickly as you can. You should not write complete sentences, since you must write quickly. When the speaker begins a new main idea, you begin a new "paragraph." Write the new idea, underline it, and then add the details.

 The following is an example of notes that a native speaker of English took while listening to the talk by Diana Soviero. Listen to the interview again, and follow along to see how these note-taking principles were followed.

The Price of Success
Schedule: exercise on stage enough, running around, and character demands
Role model: stick to it, really, really want smthg, pushed down the ladder, push back up
Wherewithal: guts, personal drive, do everything 150%, "the way I was made."

 Listen again to the interview with David King. As you listen, take notes in paragraph style on your own paper. David King speaks quickly, so it might be necessary for you to listen to the recording more than once or to stop the tape occasionally as you take notes.

After You Listen

Reorganizing Notes

David King's interview is informal. No doubt, he would organize the information in a very different way if he were giving a formal presentation titled "How to Start a Record Label."

Use the notes that you took as you listened to the interview, and complete the following outline of such a formal presentation. You may add more subpoints if you need to. Then, in a small group, retell King's story of starting a record label, using the outline that you just completed. Each group member is responsible for the information under one Roman numeral.

How to Start a Record Label

    I. Introduction: Why David King decided to start a record label

        A.   Dealing with record labels can be difficult

        B.

        C.

   II. Getting started: planning and preparation

        A.

        B.

        C.

  III. Advantages of King's partnership with Atlantic Records

        A.

        B.

        C.

  IV. Difficulties that must be overcome in running a record label

        A.

        B.

        C.

   V. Conclusion: Summary of the steps that David King took to start his record label

Pronunciation ACTIVITIES

Important Endings

In English, many words end in one or more consonants. If your native language does not have words that end in consonants, you might have to practice pronouncing these final consonants; otherwise, your listeners might misunderstand you. Compare these examples:

see   seen   Kay   Kate   go   goal   bay   bake

In addition, the ends of words often have important grammatical meanings, so all students of English need to practice some basic rules for ending pronunciation, given as follows.

Past Tense and Regular Past Participles *–ed*

When the *–ed* ending follows a voiceless consonant, it is pronounced /t/.

> **Example:** PICKED (one syllable)

When it follows a voiced consonant or a vowel, it is pronounced /d/.

> **Example:** SEEMED (one syllable)

When *–ed* follows a /t/ or /d/ sound, it is pronounced as a separate unstressed syllable.

> **Example:** WANT-ed, NEED-ed (two syllables)

Plural, Possessive, and Third Person Singular *–s* **and** *–es*

When the *–s/–es* ending follows a voiceless consonant, it is pronounced /z/.

> **Example:** MEALS (one syllable)

When it follows a voiced consonant or a vowel, it is pronounced /s/.

> **Example:** STOPS (one syllable)

When it follows the sounds /s/, /z/, /sh/, /ch/, /j/, and /zh/, it is pronounced as a separate, unstressed syllable.

> **Examples:**   GLASS-es, QUIZ-zes, PIEC-es, WISH-es, WATCH-es (two syllables)

Present Progressive, Regular Present Participle, and Gerund *–ing*

In fast, informal speech, the *–ing* ending is often pronounced *–in*. Of course, it should always be written with the correct *–ing* spelling.

> **Example:** WALK-ing   WALK-in'

Comparative and Superlative *–er* and *–est*

Each of these endings adds an additional unstressed syllable to the adjective to which it is attached.

> **Example:**   SMALL   SMALL-er   SMALL-est

Although when speaking quickly and informally people sometimes "bend" the rules for these endings, generally the *–er* and *–est* endings are used only with adjectives and adverbs of one syllable or one syllable + *–y*. Other adjectives and adverbs use the words "more" and "most" to form comparatives and superlatives. Note that you can use focal stress to give extra emphasis to the words "more" and "most."

> **Example:**   I didn't say that he was the MOST intelligent person in the world, but I DO think he's smart.

Listen to Important Endings

The following sentences from David King's interview contain many important word endings. Before you listen, underline the *–ed*, *–el–es*, *–ing*, *–er*, and *–est* endings. Then, listen and repeat after the speaker, being sure to pronounce the endings correctly.

1. The idea to start my own record label stemmed from having had bad experiences with record labels in the past.

2. In my first band, Mary's Danish, we were signed to two different labels over the course of seven years.

3. So, in my latest band, we were offered a lot of deals.

4. You can keep a band out there a lot longer and a lot happier.

5. And we walked out of the building and ended up in Rockefeller Center and looked at each other and went, "Man, what did we just do?"

6. We then hired an attorney, who handled all the legal aspects of it.

7. I mean, Atlantic pays us handsomely, is what I'm trying to say.

8. I've never worked harder in my life.

Check Your Pronunciation of Ending Consonants

Student A: Check **one** statement in each of the following pairs. Do not tell Student B which question you checked. Read it to Student B.

Student B: Listen to the statement that Student A reads. Check the appropriate ending from column two of the following list.

      After you both have completed all of the items, compare your answers. Then, reverse roles and repeat the exercise.

Student A   **Student B**

1. ____ Is that the guy who   ____ is in your English class?

    ____ Is that the guide who   ____ will show us around the museum?

2. ____ On what day are you going?   ____ On Monday

    ____ On what date are you going?   ____ On the eighteenth

3. ____ Have you seen her new play yet?   ____ Yes, I loved the acting!

    ____ Have you seen her new place yet?   ____ No, she just moved last week.

4. ____ I think I'll have Sue   ____ over for dinner.

    ____ I think I'll have soup   ____ with my salad.

5. ____ Do you know who   ____ is going with him?

    ____ Do you know whom   ____ he has asked to the dance?

Practice Pronouncing Important Endings

There are many different words or phrases that could complete the following story. Use your knowledge of English grammar to complete the following story, trying to use as many correct –ed, –s/–es, –er, –est, and –ing endings as you can. Read your story to a partner, who will write down the words and endings that he or she hears. Check to be sure that your pronunciation was clear enough for your partner to hear the endings correctly, and then listen to your partner's story and write down the words that you hear.

My friends and I love to listen to music. You can always see Joe (1) _____ the CDs in the sale rack at the local music shop. He likes to find the (2) _____ that are the (3) _____ of them all. Tiffany likes music, too, but she prefers to find new (4) _____ to listen to on the Internet. She (5) _____ it is (6) _____ than going to the store. Ivan (7) _____ music magazines that come in his mailbox every week. Last week, he read that his favorite singer will be (8) _____ in our city. I'm sure that he is (9) _____ to go to the concert. We all think this is very (10) _____ . Last summer, a group we all like (11) _____ in a city that is many (12) _____ away. Eight of us (13) _____ to go. We (14) _____ a map, and (15) _____ our travel route. The concert was (16) _____ than we expected, and we were (17) _____ . Maybe we'll all go to see Ivan's favorite singer together this summer.

Communicative Pronunciation Practice

In this interview, David King talks about his accomplishments in the music industry and how he reached his goals. To practice pronouncing important endings, tell a story of your own to a partner. Choose one of the following topics, and plan to tell your story in the past tense. You might want to record your story so that you can check your word ending pronunciation.

- My proudest moment
- An exciting event in my life
- My greatest achievement
- How I prepared myself for an important event
- A happier day than any other

TALK It Over!

Speaking Persuasively

David King talks about making his *sales pitch* to the president of Atlantic Records. A sales pitch is a persuasive presentation intended to interest a person or company in a product or service. David King's sales pitch was to encourage Atlantic Records to enter into a partnership with his record label.

Business and sales are not the only situations in which the ability to speak persuasively can be beneficial. The ability to speak persuasively can be helpful in academic and social situations as well. What other situations can you think of in which speaking persuasively could bring you benefits?

Preparing to Persuade

There are several things that you can do to plan a sales pitch or other persuasive communication. Review the following guidelines.

1. **Accentuate the Positive:** Think of all of the benefits or positive elements of your idea. You should especially consider how your idea could benefit your listener. If you are trying to convince someone to become your business partner, tell this person how your plan will bring that person profit or satisfaction.

2. **Predict Questions That Your Listener Might Ask:** If you think of the questions that you might be asked ahead of time, you can plan better answers to these questions. For example, if you are in a job interview, you can think of questions that you might be asked so that you can answer confidently and accurately about your abilities. This will make you look competent and well informed.

3. **Consider the Personal Qualities That You Have That Will Help You to Carry Out Your Plans:** Think about the list at the start of this chapter and about the unique skills, abilities, and plans that you have that will help you to complete your end of the bargain. For example, if you are persuading someone to be your partner for a business venture or a work or school project, stress the special abilities or experience that you can share with your potential partner.

4. **Predict Concerns and Reservations That Your Listener Might Have:** Think about the reasons why your listener might not agree with your ideas or plans. Then think of ways to improve either your plans or the ways in which you can address those concerns. You must be very honest with yourself in this step. For example, if you don't have the prerequisites for a class that you want to join, you must be sure to address this issue as you try to persuade the professor or teacher to let you join the class.

The following are useful phrases for addressing a listener's concerns and reservations.

- While it is true that … (I don't have the prerequisites for this course, I have studied a similar topic in another class that I took).
- I still think … (that it's worth buying the more expensive car) because (the consumer reports that I read said that I will spend less on repairs).
- You might be concerned about … but remember that …
- I admit that … is a disadvantage, but I believe that the benefits I have explained to you outweigh this one disadvantage.

Plan to Persuade

Think about David King's description of his conversation with the president of Atlantic Records. How do you think that he would follow the previous four guidelines? Fill in the following chart.

Hints for Persuading	David King's Probable Responses
Accentuate the positive	
Predict questions	
Consider your personal qualities	
Predict concerns and reservations	

TALKING POINT

Keep in mind that while words can be persuasive, body language can also be persuasive. Making eye contact and leaning forward slightly show the person you are speaking with that you are interested in them and in what they are saying.

Learn about Persuasion from Commercials

Commercials and advertisements are a special kind of persuasive communication. Advertisers use many techniques to try to persuade customers to use their product or service, including humor, facts, visual images, sounds and music, and slogans (easy-to-remember sayings).

1. With others in your class, describe commercials that you have seen that you believe are particularly persuasive. What techniques does the advertiser use to make the commercial persuasive?

2. Watch television, or listen to the radio. Listen to several commercials closely, and fill in the following chart.

3. Compare your chart with those of others in your class.

	Commercial 1	Commercial 2	Commercial 3
What is the commercial selling?			
How does it accentuate the positive?			
What benefits does it present?			
Does it address any drawbacks? How?			
What special qualities of the product are highlighted?			

You might have noticed that a commercial, which is usually over in a minute or less, does not always use all of the techniques for persuasion.

Create Your Own Commercial

With a group of classmates, plan and present a commercial for a product or service. Follow these steps.

1. Brainstorm a list of three or four products or services for which your group could make a commercial. Discuss how each of these products or services could be advertised, and then choose one.

2. Plan the format for your commercial. Use the following chart as a guide. You do not have to complete every section of the chart (or use every technique), but try to complete as many as you can.

	Your Commercial
What does the commercial sell?	
How does it accentuate the positive?	
What benefits does it present?	
Does it address any drawbacks? How?	
What special qualities of the product are highlighted?	

3. Write a script for your commercial, giving each member of your group a role to play in the commercial. Plan to use one or more persuasive advertising techniques, such as humor, facts, visual images, sound or music, and slogans.

4. Practice your commercial. Then, present the commercial to the class. If possible, make an audio or video recording of the commercial so that you can review it later and critique your ability to communicate persuasively.

Further Practice

Interviewing an Entrepreneur

Talk to someone in your community who has started a business. Find out what personal characteristics have been most helpful, what major problems have been encountered, and what advice this entrepreneur would give others who are going into business for themselves. Take notes and then report on your interview to others in your class or record your report on a tape.

Group Discussion

The ninth quality listed in the self-evaluation for entrepreneurs at the beginning of this unit is a strong desire to succeed. In a part of the interview that you did not hear, David King talks about success. Read his comments, below, and discuss the questions with a group of classmates.

> It depends on who you ask whether I'm successful. I know I am on every level. I'm successful because I'm doing what I want to do and I'm making a decent living and am really happy the majority of the time. I really enjoy what I do. But I'm not successful like STP's [Stone Temple Pilots] successful. We haven't sold millions of records. And I don't have millions of dollars. But I'm in it to win it. I love my work. We love doing this ... I'm a musician, and I realized when my first band, Mary's Danish, was on the charts and things were going well, I had this enlightening moment where I went, "Oh yeah, even if you're successful it's only about five years tops, even if you make it." So I went, "Wow, I need to branch out." Whatever I can do as long as I'm composing music and writing and playing music, I'm excited.

Discussion Questions

1. Why is it important for entrepreneurs to have a strong desire to succeed? In what other situations can a strong desire to succeed be beneficial? Is it ever harmful?

2. In David King's description of success, he talks about at least two different kinds of success. Make a list of as many different kinds of success as you can, beginning with the kinds of success that he describes. Explain how these kinds of success are different.

3. How do you think Diana Soviero would define success? Do you think that her definition of success would be the same as David King's?

4. What is your personal definition of success? What goals would you have to meet to consider yourself successful?

Chapter 7: Self-Evaluation Chart

Use the following chart to record comments about your progress in mastering each of the following skills that you practiced in this chapter.

	+	−	Teacher's Comments
Note Taking: Paragraph Notes • I understand how to use this style of note taking. • I am satisfied with my ability to use this note-taking style. • I plan to use this style again.			
Speaking Skills: Speaking Persuasively • I understand how to speak persuasively. • I am satisfied with my ability as a persuasive speaker. • I need to keep practicing these skills _____ .			
Pronunciation: Important Endings • I understand this concept. • I am satisfied with my ability to use word endings. • I will continue to practice using word endings by _____ .			

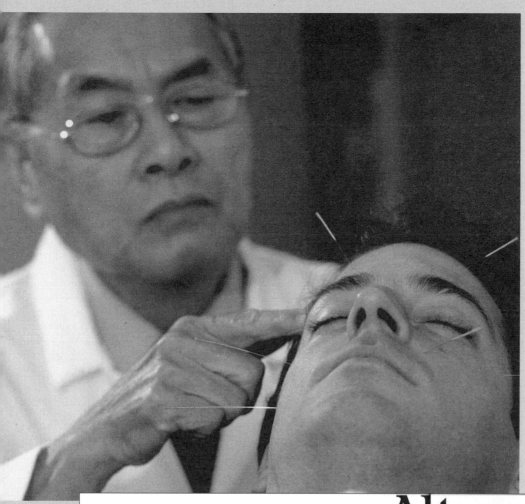

8

Alternative Medicine

CHAPTER HIGHLIGHTS

Listening	Note Taking	Pronunciation	Speaking
Main ideas Details Specific words	Getting complete information	Linking and features of fast speech	Formal presentations Fact and opinion

Brainstorming

Discuss your answers to the following questions with others in your class, or record your answers on tape.

1. Western medicine has usually relied on chemical medicines purchased in pharmacies to solve health problems. Some people are dissatisfied with these treatments and are exploring treatments from other cultures, such as acupuncture and herbal medicines which are made from plants. What type of medical treatments do you and members of your family tend to trust most?

2. What problems for doctors and patients might be associated with new types of medicines that are not yet accepted parts of conventional Western medicine?

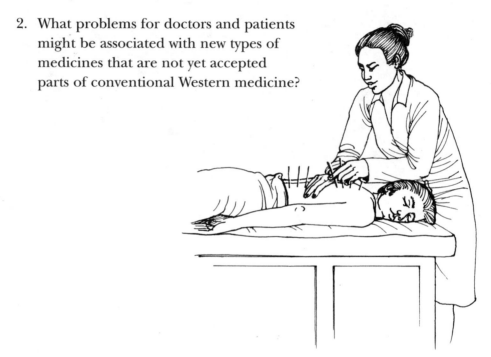

Gathering Information from Classmates

Complete the following chart with others in your class. Guess the answer if you are not sure of it, or leave a blank space if you think that there is no answer.

	Conventional Medicine	Alternative Medicine	Family or Folk Remedies
Common Cold	Rest, drink lots of fluids	Echinacea, zinc tablets, homeopathic medicine	Chicken soup
Headache			
Backache			
Weight Problem			
Asthma			
Allergy			

Listening One
Buyer Beware

Before You Listen

Some medical doctors are very open to alternative medicine, but other health care professionals are concerned that people who are desperate for cures for diseases, chronic pain, and/or weight problems might be too easily fooled into spending a lot of money on useless, even harmful, "medicines" or "treatments." The following article from the U.S. Food and Drug Administration (FDA) was written to help medical consumers make wise choices.

Read the article, and then discuss the following question.

Based on the warnings in this article, what do you think are some of the concerns that doctors and other health care professionals might have about alternative medicine?

Approaching Alternative Therapies

The National Institutes of Health (NIH) Office of Alternative Medicine recommends the following before getting involved in any alternative therapy.

- Obtain objective information about the therapy. Besides talking with the person promoting the approach, speak with people who have gone through the treatment—preferably both those who were treated recently and those treated in the more distant past. Ask about the advantages and disadvantages, risks, side effects, costs, results, and over what time span results can be expected.
- Inquire about the training and expertise of the person administering the treatment (for example, certification).
- Consider the costs. Alternative treatments might not be reimbursable by health insurance.
- Discuss all treatments with your primary care provider (usually your doctor), who needs this information in order to have a complete picture of your treatment plan.

For everyone—consumers, physicians and other health care providers, and government regulators—the FDA has the same advice when it comes to weeding out the hopeless from the hopeful: Be open-minded, but don't fall into the abyss of accepting anything at all. For there are—as there have been for centuries—countless products that are nothing more than fraud.[1]

Listen for Main Ideas

 Dr. Joseph Kornacki has several concerns about alternative medicine. He explains them in this commentary, entitled "Buyer Beware." Listen to his commentary, and list three of his concerns. Then compare your answers with a partner's.

1. _____

2. _____

3. _____

Listen for Details

Listen again to the interview with Dr. Joseph Kornacki to hear the answers to the following questions.

1. What is the one major difference between conventional medicine and most alternative medicine?

_____

2. Name two risks of getting medical treatment only from alternative medicine practitioners and not seeing a conventional doctor as well.

_____

3. How are chiropractic, physiotherapy, and acupuncture different from most other alternative medicine alternatives?

_____

4. What does Joseph Kornacki say that alternative medicine practitioners must do if they want to become an accepted part of conventional medicine?

_____

Listening Two
The New Healers

Not all doctors are as skeptical about alternative medicine as Dr. Kornacki is. Dr. Art Hister is a family practitioner and the host of a TV series about alternative medicine. Dr. Hister believes that traditional Western medicine doesn't have all of the answers and that alternative medicine can be helpful to many patients.

Before You Listen

A list of ten kinds of alternative medicine follows. Match the name of the therapy with its definition, using your knowledge of the terms or of the word parts that look familiar. For example, you might notice in the word "acupuncture" the word "puncture," meaning "to pierce or push through." Discuss your answers and what you know about these therapies with others in your class.

1. ____ acupuncture
2. ____ aromatherapy
3. ____ Aruvedic medicine
4. ____ biofeedback
5. ____ chiropractic
6. ____ herbalism
7. ____ homeopathy
8. ____ hypnotherapy
9. ____ naturopathy
10. ____ shiatsu massage

a. therapy for illness that uses only natural treatments such as diet, massage, and sunlight

b. use of herbs for medicinal purposes

c. insertion of thin needles into the body at specific points to reduce pain and inflammation

d. treatment of pain and other health problems by making suggestions to a patient under hypnosis

e. use of small amounts of a drug to treat symptoms that the drug would cause if it were taken in large doses

f. use of fragrances and smells to improve a person's mood and health

g. manipulation of the spine and muscles to help the nervous system function normally

h. use of pressure and massage on specific points on the body to relieve pain and inflammation

i. learning to voluntarily control body functions such as breathing, blood pressure, and heart rate

j. a holistic system of treatment that uses herbs, massage, and stress relievers

Listen for Specific Words

As you listen to the interview with Dr. Art Hister, mark an X next to each type of alternative medicine that is mentioned.

____ acupuncture   ____ herbalism

____ aromatherapy   ____ homeopathy

____ Aruvedic medicine   ____ hypnotherapy

____ biofeedback   ____ naturopathy

____ chiropractic   ____ shiatsu massage

Listen for Details

Listen to the interview again, and note the answers to the following questions.

1. Why are increasingly more people looking for alternative treatments for their medical problems?

   _____

2. What is the theory behind acupuncture as a therapy for pain and inflammation?

   _____

3. What is a naturopath's philosophy about why people become sick?

   _____

4. For what kinds of problems can a chiropractor be most helpful?

   _____

5. What alternative therapies has Art Hister used for his own health problems?

   _____

6. What alternative therapy is he personally most pleased with and why?

   _____

NOTE
Taking

Strategies for Getting Complete Information

When you are listening to someone talk about a topic that is not very familiar to you, you will probably not understand everything and it might be more difficult for you to take complete notes. When you find yourself in this situation, you can use the following strategies to be sure that you get the information that you need after you listen.

- When you miss a part of what a speaker says, leave a space in your notes so that you can go back later to fill in the missing information.
- Use underlining, circles, or symbols such as "?" or "/ /" to help remind yourself to fill in the missing information later.
- Write unfamiliar terms the way that they sound to you so that you can try to pronounce them when asking someone their meanings. Add the correct spellings and definitions later.
- When information is familiar, use abbreviations in your notes. This will save time for comprehension and taking notes on more-difficult material.
- When you have left spaces in your notes for missing information, go back to the notes and check the information within six hours after taking the notes. Your memory will be fresher.
- To fill in missing information, check with classmates, the professor or speaker, or library sources such as dictionaries, encyclopedias, and professional journals.

 The following is an example of notes that a native speaker of English took while listening to the talk by Joseph Kornacki. Listen to the interview again, and follow along to see how this person used note-taking strategies to help get missing information later.

Convent. Medicine open to alt. Treatment ⟶ But concerned

WHY?

In trad. Medicine treatment must be proven.

In alt med. Problem ⟶ haven't been studied

Alt Practitioners "We don't have money."

But large industry _____ ?

2nd prob. Training   ex. store workers give advice w/o train.

Some people like alt. Med. -- their problem is be-nine???? (check this!!!)

Others w/ serious illness. May not get right trad. Treatment

Some foods = harmful

    Salt can be harmful if you have _____ ???

Some alt. Therapies have professionalized

1. Chiropractors

2. ?

3. Acupun…?

Future

1. If improve standards ⟍

2. If improve training ⟋ Become part of convent. Med.

Listen to the interview with Art Hister again, and take notes on your own paper using any of the note-taking styles that you have learned. Use the strategies in the preceding box to be sure that you get complete information. After you listen, check your notes with a classmate's to fill in any missing or unclear information.

After You Listen

Consider the interviews with Dr. Hister and Dr. Kornacki. They have very different opinions about the value and safety of alternative medicine. With a group of your classmates, write at least three questions that you could ask the doctors to find out more about the information that they gave in the interview. Consider questions that ask for:

more information   proof that something is true

clarification   reasons for an opinion

_____

_____

_____

_____

_____

_____

TALKING POINT

If you had heard these talks as part of an academic class, you could bring up these questions in a discussion. If the class were a lecture class and there was no time for discussion, you could ask the questions during the professor's office hours. Professors at North American colleges and universities hold office hours so that students can ask questions like these.

Linking and Other Features of Fast Speech

In fast, everyday speech, English speakers do not pronounce every word in a sentence or phrase exactly as its pronunciation is spelled out in a dictionary. Some words are linked together, some words are shortened (or *reduced*), and some sounds are dropped, changed, or added.

Linking

Because the rhythm of spoken English demands that only the stressed syllable of a content word should receive full stress in a sentence, many other words must be reduced and linked together. Linking and blending occur when the ending sound of one word and the beginning sound of the following word are connected or combined in some way. Three common patterns of linking are described here. Notice that it is the sound of a word, and not its spelling, that determines whether the words will be linked.

Pattern 1:   The same consonant at the end of one word and the beginning of the next are linked.

> **Example:**   Often, alternative medicine practitioner**s s**pend more time with patients than doctors are able to.

Pattern 2:   The sounds /p/, /b/, /t/, /d/, /k/, and /g/ are linked to words beginning with a consonant sound.

> **Example:**   Often, alternative medicine practitioners spen**d m**ore time with patients than doctors are able to.

Pattern 3:   A word that ends in a consonant sound is linked to a word that begins with a vowel sound.

> **Example:**   Often, alternative medicine practitioners spend more time with patients than doctors a**re a**ble to.

Other Features of Fast Speech

There are many changes that happen when American English is spoken quickly. Some common ones are explained here.

- **Two Words Are Combined**

Some common word combinations are often pronounced as one word.

> **Examples:**   got to → gotta; want to → wanna; going to → gonna

Sometimes the combination causes the sounds in the words to change. This is called *assimilation,* and it is especially common when the second word begins with /y/.

> **Examples:**   don't you → dontcha; want you → wantcha;
> could you → couldja

- **Connecting Words and Prepositions Are Reduced**

Connecting words are often shortened and may even be linked to the words that precede them.

> **Examples:**   and → 'n; or → '0 r; for → fer
> of → 'a (or 'uhv before a vowel).

- **The Word Loses a Syllable (called *Ellipsis*)**

Some words actually "lose" one or more syllables in fast speech.

> **Examples:**   because → 'cause; interesting → int'resting;
> probably → prob'bly; something → somp'n

TALKING POINT

> Being aware of these changes that happen in fast speech will help you to be a better listener. You can be understood without using these features in your own speech, but students who wish to have a "native-like" accent will need to practice making these changes when they speak.

Listen to Linking and Reductions in Fast Speech

In his interview, Art Hister speaks quickly and uses many features of fast speech. Listen to the following excerpt from his interview, and mark all of the features of fast speech that you hear. You will probably need to pause the recording and listen several times so that you can listen more closely. Check your answers with a classmate's.

> I go to an acupuncturist quite regularly actually because whenever my asthma is, whenever it gets to the stage where I'm taking, uh, too much of my anti-inflammatory medications, which is one of the ways we treat those things—steroid drugs, cortisone sprays—uhm, she gives me a couple of sessions. And I have no idea if it's placebo effect, I have no idea if it's 'cause she's such a wonderful lady and I just want to get better for her, but if I go for three or four sessions, my asthma gets better and I can reduce my anti-inflammatory medications. And I'm quite happy with that.

Speaking Practice

When you are presenting information or conversing with others, you will probably not be able to think consciously about producing linking and the other features of fast speech that you have just studied. However, if you practice and try to improve the rhythm of your speech, some of these features will begin to appear in your speech naturally. If you do want to practice fast speech, try to read along while you listen to Art Hister speaking on the tape or write sentences with the example phrases given previously and record your oral practice.

TALK It Over!

Formal Presentations

You have already practiced many of the skills that you will need in order to give a formal presentation, including making an outline (Chapter 5), speaking to groups (Chapters 5 and 6), using analogies (Chapter 6), and giving definitions (Chapter 4).

Fact and Opinion in Formal Presentations

When you give a formal presentation as a student in an academic class, as a professional, or as a member of any other group, remember that you are the expert. Because people are relying on you to give accurate information, it is your responsibility to make it clear whether you are expressing fact or opinion when you speak. If you are giving your opinion, you will be most convincing if you follow your opinion with supporting facts. If you are unsure whether you are providing enough facts to support your opinion, put yourself in the position of the audience and ask critical questions of yourself.

Plan a presentation to present before your entire class. Use the following steps. Then, when you listen to classmates' presentations, take notes and ask your classmates questions. After you give your presentation, answer questions from your classmates.

1. Choose your topic. Remember that you must choose a topic that is appropriate for your audience, yet narrow enough to be covered in the time allowed. See Chapter 5 if you need guidance in choosing a topic.

2. Collect information about the topic. You probably already know a lot about the topic, if you picked something of interest to you, but you might need to collect facts to support your opinions. Use the library or the Internet to collect more information if necessary. When you give your presentation, be sure to tell the audience the source of this information.

3. Analyze the information that you collected. You might need to look at the information in several different ways until you decide on the best system of organization to clearly explain the information to your audience.

4. Write an outline to organize the parts of the information that you found during the process of analysis. You might not be able to put all of the information that you collected into a short presentation. That's alright. Choosing the most important information is part of the analysis and planning process. See Chapter 5 if you need to review outline structure.

5. Practice presenting by speaking in front of a mirror or onto tape. If you are comfortable with what you must say, you'll be able to make eye contact with your listeners and gesture naturally. You'll also be able to focus more on your pronunciation and fluency and less on the information itself.

Further Practice

Reading for More Information

Read the following article, and discuss it with a group of your classmates. (Refer to the section on discussion skills in Chapter 1 if necessary.) Then complete one or more of the activities that follow the article.

Tip-Offs to Rip-Offs

New health frauds pop up all of the time, but the promoters usually fall back on the same old clichés and tricks to gain your trust and get your money. According to the FDA, some red flags to watch out for include the following.

- Claims that the product works by a secret formula. (Legitimate scientists share their knowledge so that their peers can review their data.)
- Publicity only in the back pages of magazines, over the phone, by direct mail, in newspaper ads in the format of news stories, or thirty-minute commercials in talk show format. (Results of studies on bona fide treatments are generally reported first in medical journals.)
- Claims that the product is an amazing or miraculous breakthrough. (Real medical breakthroughs are few and far between, and when they do happen, they're not touted as "amazing" or "miraculous" by any responsible scientist or journalist.)
- Promises of easy weight loss. (For most people, the only way to lose weight is to eat less and exercise more.)
- Promises of a quick, painless, guaranteed cure.
- Testimonials from satisfied customers. (These people may never have had the disease the product is supposed to cure, may be paid representatives, or may simply not exist. Often they're identified only by initials or first names.)[2]

Activities for After You Read

1. Make a list of health frauds that you've heard about. Describe the way that these frauds were marketed and any negative effects that people have experienced because of them.

2. Search the back of magazines for advertisements like those described in the article. Check the advertisements to see which of the warning signs discussed are present.

3. Watch at least ten minutes of a television "infomercial" about a health product. (Infomercials are often listed in television schedules as "Paid Program.") As you watch, make notes of the techniques used to market the product, as well as the claims made about its usefulness. How many of the warning signs discussed previously can you find?

Role-Play

In a group of three classmates, role-play the following situations. In each, a family member has a chronic (continuous) health problem. It is not life threatening, but it does cause the person difficulty and discomfort. This family member is considering a new alternative medicine therapy that a friend used and liked. She has come to the other two group members for advice.

Situation 1

The patient is an older person who experiences muscle and joint pain. The regular doctor has prescribed pain-killers, but they don't always work. A friend has told this person about a new therapy whereby ultrasound and herbs are used to treat pain. The treatment is rather expensive, but this person is considering trying it, since nothing else has worked.

Roles: The older family member, a family member who supports the idea, and a family member who is against the idea.

Situation 2

The patient is a young person who is overweight. He has tried a variety of diets and exercise but has never been able to stick with them for more than a few weeks because he didn't see results. The weight problem makes this person insecure and unhappy a great deal of the time. A friend has told him about a camp where you spend the summer on an exercise and diet plan combined with hypnotherapy, aromatherapy, and other alternative therapies. The camp is expensive, but the patient is very anxious to lose weight and is thinking about trying it.

Roles: The young person, a family member who thinks the camp is a good idea, and a family member who thinks the camp is a bad idea.

Chapter 8: Self-Evaluation Chart

Use the following chart to record comments about your progress in mastering each of the skills that you practiced in this chapter.

	+	−	Teacher's Comments
Note Taking: Style(s) Chosen _____ • I am satisfied with my ability to use this (these) style(s) of note taking. • I am satisfied with my ability to take complete and accurate notes. • I need to keep practicing by _____ .			
Speaking Skills: Fact and Opinion/ Formal Presentations • I am satisfied with my ability to give a formal presentation. • I understand the difference between fact and opinion. • I need to continue to work on _____ .			
Pronunciation: Elements of Fast Speech • I understand these concepts. • I am satisfied with my comprehension of these elements. • I need to continue to work on _____ .			

Pairwork Pages

Chapter 4   **Communicative Pronunciation**

... and in parts of Canada

Group B

Name of the language: American Sign Language (ASL)[1]

Number of signers: 0.8% of the U.S. population.

Where used: Throughout the United States and in parts of Canada and other countries

Users: Many deaf people use ASL as their first language, some hearing people use ASL as their first language, and many hearing people know ASL as a second language.

Facts about the language: It has been used since 1817. There are many classes in which one can study ASL as a second language. Some schools and one university, Galludet University in Washington D.C., use ASL as the primary language of instruction. Although ASL is a signed language, it has different dialects just as spoken languages do.

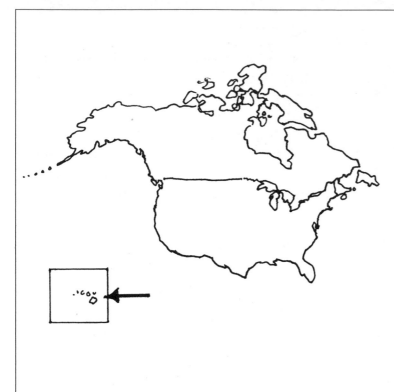

Group C

Name of the language: Hawai'i Creole English[2]

Number of speakers: 600,000 speakers (or more) in Hawai'i. 100,000 to 200,000 use Hawai'i Creole English as their only language or speak only a little English.

Speakers: The descendants of people who came to Hawai'i to work on the sugar plantations. Now many people are learning it as a second language. It is used in some Hawaiian schools, since nearly 50% of Hawaiian school children speak Hawai'i Creole English when they start school.

Resources in the language: Literature, poetry, creative writing classes, language-training tapes

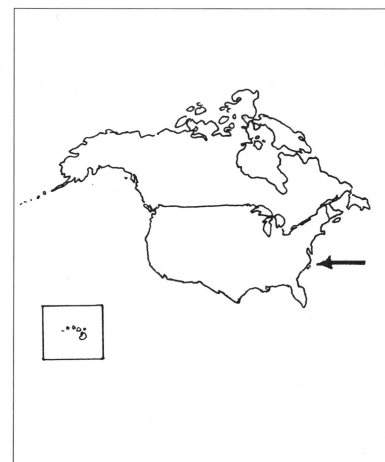

Group D

Name of the language: Sea Islands Creole English (Gullah)[3]

Number of speakers: 250,000 speakers claimed to speak Sea Islands Creole English "to some degree."

Where spoken: On the Sea Islands off the United States coast. There are also some speakers on the Atlantic coast of South Carolina, Georgia, and Florida.

Speakers: The descendants of Africans who were brought to the Americas during the slave trade

Resources in the language: Some poetry and literature have been translated into the language. Virginia Mission Geraty has written some original poetry in Gullah.

Facts about the language: There is a bilingual education program for children who speak the language. People have been predicting for over 100 years that this language will become extinct, but forms of it are still spoken.

Chapter 5 **Practice Pronouncing Focal Stress**

One partner looks at the picture on this page, and the other partner looks at the picture on page 81. The pictures are similar, but there are at least ten differences between them. Without looking at each other's pictures, each describes his or her picture and tries to locate and list the ten differences. Each should use focal stress to emphasize the differences found.

Example: A: My picture has two people at a TAble.
B: Mine TOO. My table is ROUND.
A: I have a SQUARE table.

Evaluation
Forms

Evaluation for Discussion

	4-Excellent	3-Good	2-Average	1-Needs to Improve
Evaluation of Individual Performance				
Was well prepared				
Was active participant				
Pronunciation was understandable				
Used appropriate strategies to take the floor				
Comments				
Evaluation of Group Performance				
Everyone had a chance to speak				
All group members were well prepared				
Group followed the directions				
Group came to logical and valuable conclusions				
Comments				

Evaluation for Asking and Answering Questions and Interviewing

	4-Excellent	3-Good	2-Average	1-Needs to Improve
Evaluation of Answering Questions				
Answered within three seconds				
Asked for clarification when appropriate				
Checked to be sure that the listener understood the answer				
Used appropriate statement intonation				
Comments				
Evaluation of Asking Questions				
Asked appropriate questions				
Asked for clarification if necessary				
Took notes appropriately				
Used appropriate question intonation				
Comments				

Evaluation for Defending an Opinion

	4-Excellent	3-Good	2-Average	1-Needs to Improve
Evaluation of Individual Performance				
Was well prepared				
Was an active participant				
Pronunciation was understandable				
Information was presented logically and clearly				
Evaluation of Group Performance				
Everyone had a chance to speak				
All group members were well prepared				
The group followed the directions				

Ability to defend the opinion (circle one):

5 Always able to support claims with facts, examples, and experience

4 Usually able to support claims with facts, examples, and experience

3 Had some facts, examples, and experience, but sometimes was/were unable to answer questions completely

2 Had some facts, examples, and experience to support opinions, but often not able to support opinions and give answers to questions

1 Had few facts, examples, and experience, and could not answer many questions satisfactorily

Comments

Evaluation for Presenting a Definition

	4-Excellent	3-Good	2-Average	1-Needs to Improve
Was well prepared				
Definition was clear				
Definition was complete				
Grammar of definition was accurate				
Pronunciation was understandable				

Comments

Which of the following definition techniques did the speaker use?

_____ BE verb definition

_____ Clause definition

_____ Dictionary definition (Was the name of the dictionary given? ___ yes ___ no)

_____ Word parts

_____ Examples

Evaluation for Individual and Group Presentations

	4-Excellent	3-Good	2-Average	1-Needs to Improve
Was well prepared				
Topic was interesting and appropriate				
Organization was clear and logical				
Information was complete and useful				
Pronunciation was understandable				
Body language and eye contact were appropriate				
Notes or an outline were used without distracting the audience				
Spoke with appropriate volume				
Comments				

Evaluation for Persuasive Speaking

	4-Excellent	3-Good	2-Average	1-Needs to Improve
Evaluation of Individual Performance				
Was well prepared				
Was an active participant				
Contributed to the planning of the presentation				
Pronunciation: use of thought groups and pauses				
Comments				
Evaluation of Group Performance				
All group members were well prepared				
Members accentuated the positive				
Members anticipated questions/presented benefits				
Members addressed drawbacks (might be optional)				
Comments				

Text Credits

Chapter 1

1. U.S. Census Bureau, *Statistical Abstract of the United States* (2000).

Chapter 3

1. L. Kutner, "Environmental Activism and the Internet," *Electronic Green Journal* 12 (2000) <http://egj.lib.uidaho.edu/egj12/kutner1.html>.

Chapter 4

1. SIL International, *Ethnologue: Languages of the World, 14th Ed.* (2001) <www.ethnologue.com>.
2. SIL International, *Ethnologue.*

Chapter 5

1. Adapted from: The Biotechnology Research Subcommittee, Committee on Fundamental Science and The National Science and Technology Council, *Biotechnology for the 21st Century: New Horizons* (Washington, DC: Government Printing Office, 1995): 1.
2. The Federal Coordinating Council for Science Engineering & Technology, *Biotechnology for the 21st Century: Realizing the Promise* (Washington D.C.: Office of Science & Technology Policy, 1993): 38.

Chapter 6

1. U.S. Immigration and Naturalization Service, "Statistics," (2001) <http://www.ins.usdoj.gov/graphics/aboutins/statistics/ 299.htm>.

Chapter 7

1. *Entrepreneurial Development Training Manual,* (Washington, DC: U.S. Department of Commerce, Minority Business Development Agency, 1994): 12.

Chapter 8

1. I. Stehlin, "An FDA Guide to Choosing Medical Treatments," *FDA Consumer Magazine,* 29 (1995): 13.
2. Stehlin, "An FDA Guide to Choosing Medical Treatments," 12.

Pairwork Pages

1. SIL *International, Ethnologue: Languages of the World, 14th Ed.* (2001) <www.ethnologue.com>.
2. SIL International, *Ethnologue.*
3. SIL International, *Ethnologue.*